THE AMERICAN REVOLUTION
CONSIDERED AS A SOCIAL MOVEMENT

THE
AMERICAN REVOLUTION
CONSIDERED AS
A SOCIAL MOVEMENT

BY

J. Franklin Jameson

INTRODUCTION BY ARTHUR M. SCHLESINGER

BEACON PRESS   BOSTON

Lectures delivered in November 1925 on the
Louis Clark Vanuxem Foundation

First published in 1926 in the U.S.A. by Princeton University Press;
in Great Britain by Humphrey Milford, Oxford University Press
Second printing 1940; third printing 1950
Copyright 1926 by Princeton University Press

First Beacon Paperback edition published 1956
Reprinted by arrangement with Princeton University Press

Ninth printing, October 1965

Printed in the United States of America

CONTENTS

INTRODUCTION, *by Arthur M. Schlesinger*   vii

I.   THE REVOLUTION AND THE
     STATUS OF PERSONS   3

II. THE REVOLUTION AND THE LAND   27

III. INDUSTRY AND COMMERCE   47

IV. THOUGHT AND FEELING   74

INDEX   101

INTRODUCTION

John Franklin Jameson, the author of this "small book with the big title," was little known to the public at large during his long lifetime, but among his fellow historians he enjoyed a unique reputation as a scholar's scholar. Born in 1859 in Somerville, near Boston, he received his early education at the Roxbury Latin School; then he went to Amherst College, where he graduated in 1879 with the intention of making the study and teaching of history his career. Few institutions of higher learning at the time had chairs in that field, but this did not daunt him. After a year as a high-school teacher of history at Worcester, Massachusetts, he enrolled in the newly founded Johns Hopkins University in Baltimore, where he obtained his Ph.D. in 1882, the first doctorate in history bestowed by that institution. For six years more he stayed on as a modest member of the instructional staff. In this bracing academic atmosphere the tall, slim, somewhat austere-looking youth had as his teachers, fellow students and colleagues such men of later distinction in varied fields as Woodrow Wilson, Thorstein Veblen, Richard T. Ely, Davis R. Dewey and Albert Shaw.

As an undergraduate Jameson had devoted himself to European history, but at Johns Hopkins he found his true love in the history of his own country, especially the period of its beginnings. Perhaps the nation's new pride in its past, signalized by the recurrent Revolutionary centennials commencing with the Lexington and Concord observances in 1875, unconsciously influenced his decision. Interestingly enough, he refers to these commemorations in the first essay of the present volume.

From 1888 to 1901 he served as Professor of History at Brown University and from then until 1905 in the same capacity at the University of Chicago when he left academic life to become Director of the Department of Historical Research in the Carnegie Institution of Washington, the office he held at the time he prepared the present work. Retiring in 1928 when nearing seventy, he was appointed Chief of the Division of Manuscripts in the Library of Congress and first incumbent of its newly created chair of American History. Nine years later, in 1937, while still performing these duties, he died of pneumonia.

This bald outline only faintly suggests Jameson's wide-ranging interests in the field of history and the enduring impress he made on historical scholarship in the United States. One of the original members of the American Historical Association, formed in 1884, he was thereafter perhaps its most unceasingly active and devoted member, serving as president of the organization in 1907 and as managing editor of the *American Historical Review* for nearly three decades. At the Carnegie Institution he planned and directed a priceless series of guidebooks to manuscripts and archives bearing on the American past in a dozen or more foreign countries, and as a further benefaction to specialized students he brought about the publication of numerous documentary collections on diverse historical subjects. In the case of the invaluable *Original Narratives of Early American History*, sponsored by the American Historical Association, he not only acted as the general editor but himself contributed three of the nineteen volumes.

Jameson, moreover, played a leading part in bringing to fruition the great *Dictionary of American Biography* in twenty volumes and was the prime mover in awakening the United States government to the need of adequately preserving its archival records. Happily, he lived to see the erection of the National Archives building on Pennsylvania Avenue, which, as has often been remarked, is as much a monument to Jameson as if the edifice bore his name.

Amid these multitudinous services to the cause of history Jameson found little time to distill his immense learning into books of his own authorship. Apart from two volumes on Willem Usselinx and American historiography and a potboiling *Dictionary of United States History*, all produced at Johns Hopkins or during his early Brown years, he contented himself with articles and book reviews until an invitation from Princeton University in 1925 to lecture on any subject of his choosing prompted him to compose the volume here reprinted.

The subject he chose — the social and economic meaning of the War for Independence — had long fascinated him. He had earlier discussed it in lectures delivered at Barnard College in 1895, but in the intervening thirty years scholars had devoted so little investigation to the theme that he found it necessary to make surprisingly few substantive alterations in the original manuscript. This blindness on the part of his fellow workers doubtless stemmed from their traditional absorption in political, constitutional and military history. For example, Andrew C. McLaughlin's *The Confederation and the Constitution*, a standard work on the period 1783–1789, published in 1905, confined itself almost exclusively to the governmental aspects of state and federal relations.

By 1926, however, when the Princeton University Press issued Jameson's lectures in book form, the climate of the historical profession was undergoing rapid change. A broader conception of history was emerging, a view of the American past as embracing all the concerns and activities of the people. The year before Jameson spoke at Princeton, Allan Nevins had dealt with some of the same material in his *American States Before and After the Revolution*. Within the year following the appearance of Jameson's volume Charles and Mary Beard would bring out their *Rise of American Civilization*, and the thirteen-volume co-operative *History of American Life* would commence publication.

To this school of historians *The American Revolution Considered as a Social Movement* was an epoch-marking if not epoch-making event. Beard himself hailed it as "a truly notable book." By the same token, it signaled to the public at large that eminent scholars were now taking into account the things that mattered in everyday life, with the additional attraction in this particular instance that the author expressed himself with lucidity, humor and charm.

Jameson's thoughtful work is so short and so engagingly presented that it would be a disservice to anticipate here what he has to say. No reader should deny himself the rare pleasure of perusing the book at first hand. Broadly speaking, however, the writer shows how the democratic and humane strivings attending the Revolution resulted in widening the suffrage, redistributing to smaller holders the great estates of Tory refugees, and liberalizing time-honored land-inheritance laws, and how these same influences also hastened the separation of church and state and promoted such compassionate movements as those for the restriction of Negro slavery and the slave trade. Jameson further illuminates his thesis by comparing and contrasting the American struggle for freedom with revolutionary upheavals in other countries.

With like skill he traces the effects of Independence on the whole gamut of economic life — farming, manufactures, mechanical invention, banking and finance, domestic and foreign trade — and ties these developments in with the mounting pressures for a strong federal government culminating in the Constitution. Though he notes losses as well as gains to society in the total impact of events, he devotes most attention to the constructive achievements both as being more characteristic of the era and as having more lasting results. If Jameson's many asides reveal he was writing in the aftermath of World War I, his reflections possess equal pertinence for these years following World War II, the one exception being the observation that military figures could never again play the political role they essayed after the

Revolutionary and Civil Wars, a pronouncement which obviously calls for re-examination in the light of more recent history.

Jameson does not treat every aspect of life that might have illustrated the far-reaching social significance of the Revolution. Though he touches on educational developments and the new directions in historical writing, he says nothing at all about the aspiration for an American orthography, for example, or the nationalizing impulses in painting, architecture and music, or the effort to strike down some of the outmoded concepts of the English common law. He conceived his task as primarily that of opening up "a field of history deserving further and deeper study," and a reappraisal of his performance twenty-eight years later by Frederick B. Tolles in the *American Historical Review* shows with what eagerness historical workers responded to the challenge. This abundant literature, Professor Tolles finds, though modifying some of Jameson's emphases and details and filling in some of the gaps, leaves his contribution "still vital and suggestive," "a minor classic," and "a landmark in recent American historiography."

The American Revolution Considered as a Social Movement was reprinted in 1940 and again in 1950. Now appearing under a new imprint and in a less expensive edition, this slender volume, unobtrusively informative and uncluttered with pedantry, will, it is hoped, reach a wider and long-continuing audience.

ARTHUR M. SCHLESINGER

Harvard University, 1956

THE AMERICAN REVOLUTION
CONSIDERED AS A SOCIAL MOVEMENT

I. *The Revolution and the Status of Persons*

IN this year 1925 we enter upon a long series of
celebrations commemorating the one hundred and
fiftieth anniversaries of the successive events of the
American Revolution. If any of those present are able,
like myself, to remember well the long series of centennial commemorations of those same events that marked
the years from 1875 to 1883, and even to 1889, they will,
I think, agree with me that those celebrations did more
than anything else that has happened in our life-time to
stimulate popular interest in American history in general,
and specifically in the history of the American Revolution. The *Magazine of American History* was founded
at once, in 1876. The Daughters of the American Revolution, a more numerous body than ever before were
united in the commemoration of any portion of history,
and the two societies of Sons, date from that period. A
still wider, though indirect, indication of popular his-
toric interest may be seen in the passion for what is
called "colonial" furniture, a passion which distinctly
flowed from these commemorations and especially from
the Philadelphia Centennial of 1876, for it is certain
that down to that year the sway of black walnut and
funereal horsehair was steadily maintained. A less popular but more fruitful blossoming of interest in history
may be seen in the striking rapidity with which, in the
'eighties immediately succeeding, professorships of

history were established in the American colleges and universities, and in the sudden zeal with which numbers of able young students devoted themselves to the study of their country's history.

The consequences which flowed from the celebrations of fifty years ago are so far certain to repeat themselves in our time that we may at least be sure of a speedy heightening of interest in the history of the American Revolution. The main desire that has underlain the preparation of the ensuing lectures has been the wish that whatever results, whether in learned academic research or in popular thinking, may spring from this new period of commemorations, may be marked by a wider view of the events than was taken fifty years ago. Surely it ought to be so, in view of the advances which history has made in America in fifty years, from a time when there were probably not a dozen professional students of history in the United States to a time when there are at least several hundreds.

The gain, the wider view, should show itself in three ways. In the first place, it ought to be possible for us to be much fairer to the British or Loyalist opponents of our fathers than were the men of fifty years ago. They had hardly emancipated themselves from the traditional view, generated in the heat of the old conflict, that the British statesmen of that time were monstrous tyrants, the British soldiers monstrous barbarians. There is, to be sure, an opinion abroad that the permanent maintenance of that view is an essential trait of American patriotism. It is conceded that in the study of every other war—of Athens against Sparta, or Rome against Carthage, or Parliamentarian against Royalist, or Prussia against France, or Union against Confederacy—it is the duty of rational beings to hear both sides, and not to suppose that the ultimate truth of history is to be gathered by listening solely to the immediate war-cries of one of the two contestants. An historical student who has no special affection for England, but on the other hand is not seeking any office for which he needs Irish-American votes, cannot help raising in some per-plexity the question why the common-sense rules of fairness should be inapplicable to this war alone among all wars, why our histories of it should be sedulously guarded against improvement, or why writers who take a modern and detached view of it should be accused of the covert reception of British gold.

Another advance that we ought to make consists in a revision of the popular estimate of the men of Revolu-tionary times. Fifty years ago, and even a hundred years ago, there had become fixed in the public mind the notion that, because in the period of the Revolution there were many heroic characters and deeds, the whole American population of that time was heroic. It is pleasant to think well of a whole generation of those who have preceded us, and especially pleasant to glorify them if they were our ancestors. It may seem harmless, but when it is done in terms of comparison with later generations it is not altogether wholesome. It is not wholesome because it is not just. Nothing can be more certain than that, if we consider the whole nation and not merely the individual instances of heroic character and conduct, the patriotism of 1861, on both sides, was much more widely extended and more ardent than the much-lauded patriotism of 1776, and that of 1918 more pervasive, more enlightened, and more pure than either. How could we expect it to be otherwise, when we consider carefully the circumstances of the time? Let us distinguish between the heroes who fought and suffered and made every sacrifice to bring into existence a new nation, and the population at large, of whom so great a proportion were, as a matter of fact, however we may excuse them, provincial-minded, dubious in opinion, reluctant to make any sacrifices, half-hearted in the glorious cause. All honor to the heroes, and they were many.

> We sit here in the Promised Land,
>   That flows with Freedom's honey and milk;
> But 'twas they won it, sword in hand,
>   Making the nettle danger soft for us as silk.

But let us not forget that a large part of their heroism had to be expended in overcoming difficulties which need not have existed but for the slackness and indifference of their fellows. For instance, no episode of the history of the Revolution affords a finer example of patriotic sacrifice than the winter's encampment at Valley Forge; but why were the sufferings at Valley Forge encountered? Simply because the country at large, with whatever excuses, did not support the war, and the army which was waging it, with any approach to the ardor which was shown in 1861, on both sides, or in 1918. Clothes and shoes and blankets and tents were lacking. Who does not know what would happen if an American army of the present day were found to be destitute even of chocolate drops? It would not be three days before the metropolitan dailies would be voicing loudly a nation's wrath, and car-loads of chocolate drops would be rushed promptly to every camp. Let us be fair to the moderns, and not fabricate an imaginary golden age in the undeveloped America of 1776.

Thirdly, and closer to the immediate purpose of these lectures, it is to be wished that in the coming commemorations and in our future thinking we may consider the American Revolution in broader aspects than simply the political and the military. Fifty years ago, it was these that engrossed attention, and indeed most that has been written since then about the Revolution has been narrowly confined to these two aspects, the political and the military, including of late the naval. Every move in the political struggle for independence from Great Britain, every action of the Continental Congress, has been described over and over again. Every battle and every skirmish in that long and dragging war has had its historian, or has been the theme of meticulous articles or controversial pamphlets. Meanwhile, even in this age when social history is so much in fashion all over the world, few writers have concerned themselves with the social aspects of our American revolutionary history.

How different is it with the Frenchmen's study of the great French Revolution! Forty or fifty years ago they were in much the same state as we: every move of the politicians, every picturesque happening in Paris, every march or engagement of the revolutionary armies, was eagerly chronicled by intelligent but more or less conventional historians; but in more recent years the horizon of the French historians of their revolution has broadened, and more attention has been given to the prodigious effects of the French Revolution upon the constitution of French society than to the political events, more to the march of the revolutionary ideas than to the march of the revolutionary battalions, and quite as much to the progress of the revolution in the provinces as to the dramatic events that marked its development in Paris. The result has been that the French Revolution is now seen in its true proportions and effects, not simply as the downfall of monarchy or the securing of equal political rights for all individuals, but chiefly as a social movement, French and European, of vast dimensions and of immense significance.

Perhaps some may be moved to say at once: But this is precisely to ignore the most salient contrast between the American Revolution and the French. The men of our Revolution, they will say, were neither levellers nor theorists. Their aims were distinctly political, not social. They fought for their own concrete rights as Englishmen, not for the abstract rights of man, nor for liberty, equality, and fraternity. The French rose in revolt against both a vicious political system and a vicious social system. With enthusiastic ardor they proceeded to sweep away abuses of all sorts, and to create, not simply a new government, but a new France and indeed, to their own imaginations, a new heaven and a new earth. That they cared more for the social than for the political results of the Revolution was evident when, after a few years, believing it impossible to retain both, they resigned political freedom and threw themselves into the arms of the young Corsican who gave promise of preserving for them their new social system. Not so, it will be said, the Anglo-Saxon. He had no wish to destroy or to recast his social system. He sought for political freedom, but he had no mind to allow revolution to extend itself beyond that limited sphere. As Burke said, he was "taught to look with horror on those children of their country who are prompted rashly to hack that aged parent to pieces and put him into the kettle of magicians, in hopes that by their poisonous weeds and wild incantations they may regenerate the paternal constitution."

It is indeed true that our Revolution was strikingly unlike that of France, and that most of those who originated it had no other than a political programme, and would have considered its work done when political independence of Great Britain had been secured. But who can say to the waves of revolution: Thus far shall we go and no farther? The various fibres of a nation's life are knit together in great complexity. It is impossible to sever some without also loosening others, and setting them free to combine anew in widely different forms. The Americans were much more conservative than the French. But their political and their social systems, though both were, as the great orator said, still in the gristle and not yet hardened into the bone of manhood, were too intimately connected to permit that the one should remain unchanged while the other was radically altered. The stream of revolution, once started, could not be confined within narrow banks, but spread abroad upon the land. Many economic desires, many social aspirations were set free by the political struggle, many aspects of colonial society profoundly altered by the forces thus let loose. The relations of social classes to each other, the institution of slavery, the system of land-holding, the course of business, the forms and spirit of the intellectual and religious life, all felt the transforming hand of revolution, all emerged from under it in shapes advanced many degrees nearer to those we know.

These are only assertions. They cannot be adequately proved in a few lectures. It will content the lecturer if he can partially illustrate their truth, and if some who hear him are convinced that here is a field of history deserving further and deeper study. Meantime we might profitably consider for a moment whether it is intrinsically probable that our revolution was unlike other popular revolutions, in having no social results flowing from the political upheaval. Is there such a thing as a natural history of revolutions? Nation differs from nation, and age from age, but there are some uniformities in human nature, some natural sequences recurrently presenting themselves in human history. Not all political revolutions, it is true, have had important social consequences. One notable variety of revolution is that whereby one reigning individual or one small group of individuals holding supreme power is supplanted by another individual or small group, without any serious alteration of the system. Such are those "palace revolutions" whereby Jehu the son of Nimshi succeeds Jehoram the son of Ahab, or the tsar Alexander supplants the tsar Paul, without more disturbance of the social system than when "Amurath to Amurath succeeds" in a wholly peaceable manner. But it is the other variety, popular revolutions, which we have in mind. This is the variety which figures most largely in modern history. A popular revolution usually consists in the transfer of political power from the hands of a smaller into those of a larger mass of the citizens, or from one great section of the population to another. As the result of such a revolution, we expect to see the new group exercising its new-found power in accordance with its own interests or desires, until, with or without fixed intention of so doing, it alters the social system into something according better with its own ideals. After

the peaceful English revolution known as the passing of
the Parliamentary Reform Act of 1832, we look to see
the new Parliament, chosen by a wider suffrage and
representing now the middle classes, passing a mass of
legislation that brings the social state of England into
better conformity with middle-class ideals. After the
American Civil War, which shifted the seat of political
power from the planting aristocracy of the South to the
manufacturing and commercial classes of the North, we
look to see legislation and the growth of custom whereby
the American social system takes on forms congenial to
the minds of the new possessors of power. But indeed
we do not need to look farther into the past than the
last nine years, to observe how the greatest of all revolutions, the one destined evidently to be the most
momentous in its consequences, beginning with the overthrow of a tsar and the substitution of a republic,
speedily escapes from the control of those who would
keep it purely or mainly political, and transforms Russian society by 1925 to an extent which no one would in
1913 have dreamed to be possible.

If then it is rational to suppose that the American
Revolution had some social consequences, what would
they be likely to be? It would be natural to reply that
it depends on the question, who caused the Revolution,
and that therefore it becomes important to inquire
what manner of men they were, and what they would
be likely, consciously or unconsciously, to desire.
In reality, the matter is not quite so simple as that.
Allowance has to be made for one important fact in the
natural history of revolutions, and that is that, as they
progress, they tend to fall into the hands of men holding
more and more advanced or extreme views, less and less

restrained by traditional attachment to the old order of things. Therefore the social consequences of a revolution are not necessarily shaped by the conscious or unconscious desires of those who started it, but more likely by the desires of those who came into control of it at later stages of its development.

You know how it was with the English Revolution of the seventeenth century. At first it was the affair of moderate statesmen, like Pym and Hampden, or moderate generals like Essex or Manchester, earls, who would not push the king too hard, but before long it fell into the hands of men like Cromwell, whose spirit is shown by his bold declaration, "If I should meet the king in battle, I would as soon fire my pistol at him as at any man." Now when we examine the interesting mass of constitutional and social legislation enacted by the parliaments of the Commonwealth, we see in it the work of men of far more advanced views than those of Pym and Hampden, to wit, of radicals who had come into control of the movement in its latest stages.

Or again, take the French Revolution. Everyone knows how its history is marked by distinct successive periods, in each of which the control is exercised by a group more radical and extreme than its predecessors; and the same has been true of the great Russian revolution. Now, widely as our American Revolution differed from these, do not let us suppose that it escaped every trait of conformity to the natural history of such movements. Certain it is that, in some of our states at least, it fell ultimately into quite other hands than those that set it in motion.

Well, then, we may ask, who were in favor of the Revolution, and who were against it? The answer of course varies with the different stages of its development. In 1774 the partisans of American independence were very few, though there had long been those who thought, in an academic way, that it would soon take place. In most years after 1776 the partisans of American independence were the great majority. But what sort of man became a Tory as it gradually became necessary to take sides? What sort of man became a Whig? As a matter of course, almost all persons who enjoyed office under the Crown became Tories, and these were a large number. In an age when the king's turnspit was a member of Parliament, and under a king whose chief means of political action was the distribution of offices, office-holders were certain to be numerous, and their pay was, in proportion to the wealth of the country and the work they had to do, much greater than it is now. If the natural desire of all mankind to hold on to a lucrative office (a desire which is said sometimes to influence political action even in this age) did not make an office-holder a Tory, there was another motive arising from the fact that he had been appointed and had sworn to execute the laws, and might therefore feel in duty bound to obey the instructions, of the ministers in England. As for the merchants, many, who had extensive interests that were imperilled by rebellion, adhered to the royal cause. But on the whole the great body of the merchants of the thirteen colonies were Whigs, for of the deep underlying causes, which for a generation had been moving the American mind in the direction of independence, none was so potent, according to all the best testimony, as the parliamentary restrictions on the trade of the colonies. Among farmers many of the richest took the royalist side. Probably most Episcopalians did so, except in the South. Everywhere the debtor class was, as was natural, and as has been true the whole world over, mainly on the side of revolution.

If we speak of professions, we should note that probably most of the clergy were Whigs, with the exception of nearly all the clergymen of the Church of England in the northern colonies. Most lawyers were Whigs, but most of the most eminent and of those enjoying the largest practice were Tories. John Adams says that, of the eight lawyers who had an important practice before the Superior Court of Massachusetts at the time of the Stamp Act, only Otis and he were Whigs ten years later. One of the others had died, and the remaining five were Tories. Among physicians the proportion of Tories was quite as large as among lawyers.

A word as to race and nationality. Colonists who had very recently arrived from England were likely to take the Tory side. Immigrants from Scotland, also, were usually Tories. A hundred and fifty years ago the Scots at home were among the warmest of Tories; Hume's *History of England* is typical of their feelings. Perhaps, too, their well-known clannishness gave them, in America, the position of aliens who held together, and would not assimilate with the rest of the population. Of the Irish, on the other hand, and those of the Scotch-Irish stock, Protestants from the north of Ireland, it is customary to hold that they were warmly and by vast majority on the side of revolution. It is not so certain. Industrious efforts have been made to show that they formed the backbone of the Revolutionary army— efforts partly based on a misinterpretation of a single passage in Joseph Galloway's testimony before a committee of the House of Commons. On the other hand, I have observed that, in the two large lists of Loyalist claimants that give the country of birth, 146 out of 1358 claimants, or eleven per cent, say that they were born in Ireland—a larger number than were born in England. Yet in Pennsylvania, where the proportion of Irish or Scotch-Irish population was greatest, it was unquestionably their influence that carried the state for independence, at the same time breaking the power in state affairs of the Philadelphia conservatives, and bestowing upon the state a radically democratic constitution. In all the colonies the Germans generally adhered to the party of independence, but not with great ardency.

As is usually the case, the revolutionary side was more frequently espoused by young men, the conservative cause by their elders. There were not a few conspicuous cases, such as that of Sir John Randolph, the king's attorney-general in Virginia, and his son Edmund Randolph, in which the son adopted the former, the father the latter cause, and other cases, like that of Samuel and Josiah Quincy, in which an elder and a younger brother were thus divided. Among all the leaders of the Revolution, very few were forty-five years old in 1775; most were under forty. But think for a moment of the leaders of the French Revolution— Robespierre thirty-one years old when the Revolution began, Danton thirty, Camille Desmoulins twenty-seven, Collot-d'Herbois thirty-nine, Couthon thirty-three, Lebas twenty-four, Saint-Just twenty-one—and we shall see cause to be glad that our Revolution was carried through by men who, though still young, had at any rate reached their full maturity of thought and of character.

If we should investigate the Tory party in the several colonies in detail, we should be forced to the conviction that, in New England, it comprised in 1775 a very great share, probably more than half, of the most educated, wealthy, and hitherto respected classes. In March 1776, when Howe evacuated Boston, eleven hundred refugees sailed away with him. These eleven hundred, and the thousand or more who subsequently followed them, bore away perhaps a majority of the old aristocracy of Massachusetts. The act of banishment which the state legislature passed in 1778, to punish the Tories, includes among its three hundred-odd names some representatives of most of the families which had been distinguished in the earlier days of the colony. The loss of this important element, cultivated, experienced, and public-spirited, was a very serious one. It is true that many Tories returned after the war, but their fortunes were usually much broken, and they could never regain their influence. In New England, in short, it appears that the Revolution brought new strata everywhere to the surface.

In New York it seems probable that, in the height of the war at least, the bulk of the property-owners belonged to the Tory party, and it was strong also among the middle classes of the towns and among the country population. On the large manorial estates the tenant farmers sided with their landlords if they took sides at all. The city of New York and the county of Westchester were strongly Tory during at least the period of the British occupation, and Westchester very likely before. So were Staten Island and the three counties of Long Island.

In Pennsylvania it is probable that during the critical years of the war, at least, the majority of the population was on the side of the Crown, and that majority seems to have included many persons of eminence, and many Quakers. On the other hand, as is well known, the Virginian aristocracy in general, living somewhat remote from the influence of the royal officials, upon their secluded estates, were full of the spirit of local independence. Quite unlike their New England compeers, they took the Whig side, and that almost unanimously. It was the Virginian planters who formed the local committees, seized from the outset the control of the movement, and made it impossible for loyalty to show itself in concerted or effective action. And it is well known how numerous and active were the Tories in the Carolinas. But, says Dr. Ramsay, speaking of South Carolina, "Beside their superiority in numbers, there was an ardour and enthusiasm in the friends of Congress which was generally wanting in the advocates for royal government." Is not this a most significant touch? After all the evidence as to classes and numbers—for perhaps there were a hundred thousand Loyalist exiles, to say nothing of the many more who did not emigrate—the ultimate success of the American cause might well seem to us a miracle. But the fact remains that the Revolutionary party knew what they wanted. They had a definite programme, they had boldness and resolution, while those averse to independence were divided in their counsels, and paralyzed by the timidity which naturally cleaves to conservative minds. The first scientific observer of political revolutions, Thucydides, pointed out, and every subsequent revolution has accentuated his words, that in such times boldness and energy are more important requisites to success than intelligence or all other qualities put together. This is the secret of the whole matter. "There was an ardour and enthusiasm in the friends of Congress which was generally wanting in the advocates for royal government."

All things considered, it seems clear that in most states the strength of the revolutionary party lay most largely in the plain people, as distinguished from the aristocracy. It lay not in the mob or rabble, for American society was overwhelmingly rural and not urban, and had no sufficient amount of mob or rabble to control the movement, but in the peasantry, substantial and energetic though poor, in the small farmers and frontiersmen. And so, although there were men of great possessions like George Washington and Charles Carroll of Carrollton who contributed a conservative element, in the main we must expect to see our social changes tending in the direction of levelling democracy.

It would be aside from the declared purpose of these lectures to dwell upon the political effects which resulted from the victory of a party constituted in the manner that has been described. There are, however, some political changes that almost inevitably bring social changes in their wake. Take, for instance, the expansion of the suffrage. The status in which the electoral franchise was left at the end of the Revolutionary period fell far short of complete democracy. Yet during the years we are considering the right of suffrage was much extended. The freeholder, or owner of real estate, was given special privileges in four of the new state constitutions, two others widened the suffrage to include all owners of either land or personal property to a certain limit, and two others conferred it upon all tax-payers. Now if in this lecture we are considering especially the status of persons, we must take account of the fact that the elevation of whole classes of people to the status of voters elevates them also in their social status. American society in the colonial period had a more definite and stable organization than it ever has had since the Revolution. It had been like that English county society of which the poet speaks,

> Where Aylmer followed Aylmer at the hall,
> And Averill Averill at the rectory.

Now, multitudes of squires had been driven into exile or dethroned from their high position of dominance over the community. Multitudes of other Loyalists had been disfranchised, or impoverished by confiscations. Rip Van Winkle, whose sleep bridged just these years, found the atmosphere of his village radically altered. Jeremy Belknap of New Hampshire, writing in 1792, after remarking on the effect of the Revolution in calling the democratic power into action and repressing the aristocratic spirit, confesses that in the new state "the deficiency of persons qualified for the various departments in the Government has been much regretted, and by none more than by those few who know how public business ought to be conducted." In that entertaining Virginian autobiography, the *Life* of the Reverend Devereux Jarratt, after speaking of the habit in that writer's youth, among the plain people with whom he grew up, of regarding gentle-folk as beings of a superior order, he says in 1794:

But I have lived to see a vast alteration in this respect and the contrary extreme prevail. In our high republican times there is more levelling than ought to be, consistent with good government.

I have as little notion of oppression and tyranny as any man, but a due subordination is essentially requisite in every government. At present there is too little regard and reverence paid to magistrates and persons in public office; and whence do this regard and irreverence originate but from the notion and practice of levelling? An idea is held out to us that our present government and state are far superior to the former, when we were under the royal administration; but my age enables me to know that the people are not now by half so peacefully and quietly governed as formerly; nor are the laws, perhaps by the tenth part, so well executed. And yet I know the superiority of the present government. In theory it is certainly superior; but in practice it is not so. This can arise from nothing so much as from want of a proper distinction between the various orders of the people.

Similar voices come from North Carolina, where one stout conservative laments the "extension of that most delicate and important right [of suffrage] to every biped of the forest," and another declares that: "Anyone who has the least pretence to be a gentleman is suspected and borne down *per ignobile vulgus*—a set of men without reading, experience, or principle to govern them." In fact, the sense of social change pervaded the country. A writer in South Carolina says, quite in the spirit of these lectures, "There is nothing more common than to confound the terms of the American Revolution with those of the late American war. The American war is over, but this is far from being the case with the American revolution. On the contrary, nothing but the first act of the great drama is closed."

The workings of the popular sentiment in favor of equality may of course be plainly seen in the legislation abolishing rights of primogeniture and distributing more or less equally the estates of persons dying intestate, but this movement may perhaps be more conveniently considered in a lecture devoted to the Revolution and the

Land. We might also expect the equalitarian or humane spirit to show itself in alterations of the laws respecting redemptioners or indented servants. Those laws, however, seem not to have been changed in the Revolutionary period. We may infer that the laws protecting the interests of such persons, a very numerous class in the years just preceding the Revolution, either were, or were deemed to be, adequate already for their humane purpose, and that the status of the indented, who after all had but a few years to serve and then would have all the rights of other poor people, was not regarded as seriously unsatisfactory.

A far more serious question, in any consideration of the effect of the American Revolution on the status of persons, is that of its influence on the institution of slavery, for at this time the contrast between American freedom and American slavery comes out, for the first time, with startling distinctness. It has often been asked: How could men who were engaged in a great and inspiring struggle for liberty fail to perceive the inconsistency between their professions and endeavors in that contest and their actions with respect to their bondmen? How could they fail to see the application of their doctrines respecting the rights of man to the black men who were held among them in bondage far more reprehensible than that to which they indignantly proclaimed themselves to have been subjected by the King of Great Britain?

At the time when the Revolution broke out there were about a half-million of slaves in the Thirteen Colonies, the figures probably running about as follows: 200,000 in Virginia, 100,000 in South Carolina, 70,000 or 80,000 each in Maryland and in North Carolina, 25,000 perhaps in New York, 10,000 in New Jersey, 6,000 in Pennsylvania, 6,000 in Connecticut, 5,000 in Massachusetts, 4,000 in Rhode Island. Slavery in the continental colonies at that time was no doubt less harsh than in the West Indies, and milder than it has been in many other countries and times. An English parson, preaching to a Virginian congregation in 1763, says: "I do you no more than justice in bearing witness, that in no part of the world were slaves ever better treated than, in general, they are in the colonies." But slavery is slavery, and already before the Revolution many hearts had been stirred against it. It is of course true that other influences than those of the American Revolution were abroad in the world at the same time which would surely work in some degree against the institution of human slavery. On the one hand Voltaire had raised a powerful, if at times a grating, voice in favor of a rational humanitarianism, and Rousseau had poured upon time-worn institutions the active solvent of abounding sentimentality. Quite at another extreme of human thought from them, Wesley and Whitefield had stirred the English nation into a warmth of religious feeling of which Methodism was only one result, and with it came a revived interest in all varieties of philanthropic endeavor.

There is no lack of evidence that, in the American world of that time, the analogy between freedom for whites and freedom for blacks was seen. If we are to select but one example of such evidence, the foremost place must surely be given to the striking language of Patrick Henry, used in 1773, when he was immersed in the struggle against Great Britain. It is found in a letter which he wrote to one who had sent him a copy of Anthony Benezet's book on slavery.

Is it not amazing [he says] that at a time, when the rights of humanity are defined and understood with precision, in a country above all others fond of liberty, that in such an age and in such a country we find men professing a religion the most humane, mild, gentle and generous, adopting a principle as repugnant to humanity as it is inconsistent with the Bible and destructive to liberty? . . . Would anyone believe I am the master of slaves of my own purchase! I am drawn along by the general inconvenience of living here without them. I will not, I can not justify it. However culpable my conduct, I will so far pay my devoir to virtue, as to own the excellence and rectitude of her precepts, and lament my want of conformity to them. I believe a time will come when an opportunity will be offered to abolish this lamentable evil. Everything we can do is to improve it, if it happens in our day, if not, let us transmit to our descendants, together with our slaves, a pity for their unhappy lot, and an abhorrence of slavery. . . . It is a debt we owe to the purity of our religion, to show that it is at variance with that law which warrants slavery.

Along with many examples and expressions of individual opinion, we may note the organized efforts toward the removal or alleviation of slavery manifested in the creation of a whole group of societies for these purposes. The first anti-slavery society in this or any other country was formed on April 14, 1775, five days before the battle of Lexington, by a meeting at the Sun Tavern, on Second Street in Philadelphia. The members were mostly of the Society of Friends. The organization took the name of "The Society for the Relief of Free Negroes unlawfully held in Bondage." In the preamble of their constitution they point out that "loosing the bonds of wickedness and setting the oppressed free, is evidently a duty incumbent on all professors of Christianity, but more especially at a time when justice, liberty, and the laws of the land are the general topics among most ranks and stations of men." The New York "Society for Promoting the Manumission of Slaves" was organized in 1785, with John Jay for its first president. In 1788 a society similar to these two was founded in Delaware, and within four years there were other such in Rhode Island, Connecticut, New Jersey, Maryland, and Virginia, and local societies enough to make at least thirteen, mostly in the slave-holding states.

In actual results of the growing sentiment, we may note, first of all, the checking of the importation of slaves, and thus of the horrors of the trans-Atlantic slave trade. The Continental Congress of 1774 had been in session but a few days when they decreed an "American Association," or non-importation agreement, in which one section read: "That we will neither import nor purchase any slave imported after the first day of December next, after which we will wholly discontinue the slave trade, and will neither be concerned in it ourselves, nor will we hire our vessels nor sell our commodities or manufactures to those who are concerned in it"; and the evidence seems to be that the terms of this agreement were enforced throughout the war with little evasion.

States also acted. Four months before this, in July 1774, Rhode Island had passed a law to the effect that all slaves thereafter brought into the colony should be free. The influence under which it was passed may be seen from the preamble. "Whereas," it begins, "the inhabitants of America are generally engaged in the preservation of their own rights and liberties, among which that of personal freedom must be considered as the greatest, and as those who are desirous of enjoying all the advantages of liberty themselves should be willing to extend personal liberty to others," etc. A similar law was passed that same year in Connecticut. Delaware prohibited importation in 1776, Virginia in 1778, Maryland in 1783, South Carolina in 1787, for a term of years, and North Carolina, in 1786, imposed a larger duty on each negro imported.

Still further, the states in which slaves were few proceeded, directly as a consequence of the Revolutionary movement, to effect the immediate or gradual abolition of slavery itself. Vermont had never recognized its existence, but Vermont was not recognized as a state. Pennsylvania in 1780 provided for gradual abolition, by an act which declared that no negro born after that date should be held in any sort of bondage after he became twenty-eight years old, and that up to that time his service should be simply like that of an indented servant or apprentice. Now what says the preamble of this act? That when we consider our deliverance from the abhorrent condition to which Great Britain has tried to reduce us, we are called on to manifest the sincerity of our professions of freedom, and to give substantial proof of gratitude, by extending a portion of our freedom to others, who, though of a different color, are the work of the same Almighty hand. Evidently here also the leaven of the Revolution was working as a prime cause in this philanthropic endeavor.

The Superior Court of Massachusetts declared that slavery had been abolished in that state by the mere declaration of its constitution that "all men are born free and equal." In 1784 Connecticut and Rhode Island passed acts which gradually extinguished slavery. In other states, ameliorations of the law respecting slaves were effected even though the abolition of slavery could not be brought about. Thus in 1782 Virginia passed an act which provided that any owner might, by an instrument properly attested, freely manumit all his slaves, if he gave security that their maintenance should not become a public charge. It may seem but a slight thing, this law making private manumission easy where before it had been difficult. But it appears to have led in eight years to the freeing of more than ten thousand slaves, twice as great a number as were freed by reason of the Massachusetts constitution, and as many as there were in Rhode Island and Connecticut together when the war broke out.

That all was not done that might have been done for the removal or amelioration of slavery we cannot deny, nor that there was in many places a glaring contrast between the principles avowed by the men of the Revolution and their acts respecting slavery; yet very substantial progress was made, and that more was made in this period than in any other until a much later time may be taken as clear evidence of a pronounced influence of the Revolution upon the status of persons in the realm where that status stood most in need of amelioration.

Thus in many ways the successful struggle for the independence of the United States affected the character of American society by altering the status of persons. The freeing of the community led not unnaturally to the freeing of the individual; the raising of colonies to the position of independent states brought with it the promotion of many a man to a higher order in the scale of privilege or consequence. So far at any rate as this aspect of life in America is concerned, it is vain to think of the Revolution as solely a series of political or military events.

II. *The Revolution and the Land*

IT would appear from the satirical remarks of
Dickens and others that, eighty years ago, the first
question asked of a European visitor to any part of
the United States was, "How do you like our institutions?" Our institutions, especially the institutions of
democracy, were thought of as the most notable posses-
sion or attribute of the United States, and many indeed
seem to have regarded them as the source of all our
prosperity and prospects of advancement.

But during the past fifty years historians have not
been idle, and, though it runs counter to many con-
temptuous or patronizing declarations that I see in
print, to me they seem to have been doing their work
with a certain degree of intelligence. In particular, they
have been much impressed with the thought that the
average man, in all ages, has been more occupied with
making a living than with any other one thing. This has
led them to doubt whether economic phenomena are
not more often the cause than the effect of political institutions and arrangements, and in the case of American history to question closely the view that our political
institutions are the source from which all blessings flow.

The doctrine which underlies the present lecture is
that political democracy came to the United States as a
result of economic democracy, that this nation came
to be marked by political institutions of a democratic
type because it had, still earlier, come to be characterized in its economic life by democratic arrangements

and practices. We do not look to see effects precede causes, and certainly political democracy came among us somewhat late, certainly long after the Revolution in most states. If we take manhood suffrage as the most convenient symbol of political democracy, we have to say that it was 1840 before manhood suffrage came at all close to being the universal rule of American political life. Long before this, however, America stood committed to economic democracy, which meant, in a country so occupied with agriculture, to the system of landholding which the classical economists called "peasant proprietorship," the system of small holdings where landowner, capitalist or farmer, and laborer are all one, the owner of the land supplying the capital and working the fields with his own labor and that of his family.

It is difficult for us now to imagine a country so entirely rural as was the America of a hundred and fifty years ago. The population was sparse, but that does not tell the whole story. There are parts of the country now, even in the regions east of the Mississippi, that are thinly settled. But none of them lies outside the sphere of influence of a large city, and most of them have cities and large towns near at hand. Almost half of our whole vast population dwells in towns of more than 8,000 inhabitants. Now when the Revolution began there were in all the thirteen colonies but five towns of that size, and only two or three per cent of the people lived in them. From the pastures of Maine to the rice-fields of Georgia, America was almost absolutely rural, and her people were almost wholly devoted to agriculture. We hear much of the commerce, the fisheries, and the manufactures of New England. Dr. Franklin, some years

[28]

after the war, declared roundly that these occupations did not engross the time and capital of more than a tenth as many New Englanders as were occupied with agriculture. Much more in other colonies must it have dominated all other pursuits. If this be so, it needs no demonstration that the relations of the American to the land were of the very first consequence. Therefore, in our study of the social changes which accompanied and followed upon the American Revolution, we may properly give a place of great prominence to the land. Is there indeed any portion of American history in which we get far away from that primary relationship? "Land," was the first cry of the wave-tossed mariners of Columbus; land-hunger among the crowded inhabitants of western Europe was the chief impulse toward the colonization of the New World; and in all times till quite lately the chief task of American manhood has been this, to go up against the land and possess it, to subdue the continent, to win for mankind its primary victory over the elemental forces of nature. Under what forms of organization these battles should be won was of the first consequence to the future of the country and of the world. Naturally, the first attacks were made under forms derived from the Old World. Chartered companies were given extensive grants of the soil. Lords of the council, whom spendthrift monarchs had not the means to reward properly in England for zealous services to the Crown, were appeased by vague grants of territories in the American wilderness. It was all so unknown that the grants might perchance overlap each other, but there was probably something over there out of which a courtier could make something. Hence those strange paraphernalia of palatines and landgraves and admirals and chamberlains and chancellors with which the proprietors of Carolina decorated and burdened their infant province—"thrones, dominions, principalities, and powers," but few inhabitants. Elsewhere, perhaps, manors were erected, with courts baron and courts leet and all the machinery of English estates. Upon the Hudson River the Dutch West India Company established patroons, with almost regal rights over great feudal principalities, so extensive as quite to overshadow the settlements of lesser folk.

But if we bring up before our minds the familiar map of the Atlantic portions of the United States, we see at a glance that there was a marked difference between the physical geography of the northern and the southern regions of that coast. In the north the mountains and the foot-hills that spread out before them come close to the sea, and the river-courses are troubled, but a few miles back from the coast, by rapids and waterfalls. Here, therefore, the settler, if he would have a market in those days of water-transportation, must live near the sea. The soil, too, uneven and unfertile, was such as could be profitably worked only by one who gave his personal attention to a small area of it. Here, therefore, compact settlement was the rule, and large estates were likely to be the exception—that is to say, large estates of cultivated land, for there was nothing to make it difficult for one man to hold great tracts of forest, or wild lands of the interior. But as one goes southward the mountains recede from the coast. The alluvial belt grows broader. Long navigable rivers penetrate the country, such as those which divide Virginia into long and narrow peninsulas. Here the English immigrant could indulge to the full his natural English propensity

toward a large estate of land and a life properly separated
from that of his fellows. All around his home, too, the
land lay in great levels which could profitably be man-
aged upon a large scale and by the labor of hired servants
or slaves. While, then, New England had few large
estates, and its aristocracy was chiefly urban, throughout the rest of the country the English system of large
properties was extensively followed. There were large
manors in New York and Pennsylvania and Maryland,
estates embracing thousands of acres each in Virginia
and the colonies farther southward. The manorial grants
in New York embraced more than two and a half million
acres. In 1769 it was estimated that at least five-sixths
of the inhabitants of Westchester County lived within
the confines of the great manors there, and the great
Van Rensselaer manor, a hundred miles farther up the
Hudson, covered an area of twenty-four miles by twenty-
eight, two-thirds the size of Rhode Island. The Fairfax
estate in Virginia at one time embraced six million
acres; that of Lord Granville in North Carolina included
at least a third of the colony.

But all this was, as has been hinted, a European system transplanted to the New World. It was not native
here, and in some respects it was not natural, nor well
suited to American conditions of life. It would do very
well for certain alluvial districts of the Atlantic region,
but it would not do at all for the broad belt of hilly and
mountainous country which lay next to the westward.
Yet to attack that uneven region and subdue it to the
purpose of man was the next task which lay before the
eager and indomitable American spirit. The English
system of land-tenure had well enough served the uses
of America thus far, perhaps, but it would not serve

them much longer. Its hold upon America was loose. If anything should occur which should administer a great shock to the entire social system of the country, it would dislodge and shake off from the body politic, as an outworn vesture, such institutions as no longer met our needs. Now this is just what the Revolution did. It broke up so much that was traditional and customary with the Americans, in dissolving their allegiance to a monarchy for which they had felt a most loyal attachment, that whatever else was outgrown or exotic seemed to be thrown into the melting-pot, to be recast into a form better suited to the work which the new nation had before it. The hot sun of revolution withered whatever was not deeply rooted in the soil. There was no violent outbreak against the land-system, for there had been no grinding oppressions or exactions connected with it. No maddened and blood-stained peasants rushed furiously from château to château, burning court-rolls and shedding the blood of seigneurs and châtelains. But in a quiet, sober, Anglo-Saxon way a great change was effected in the land-system of America between the years 1775 and 1795.

In the first place, royal restrictions on the acquisition of land fell into abeyance. The king's proclamation of 1763, forbidding settlement and the patenting of lands beyond the Alleghenies, and those provisions of the Quebec Act of 1774 which in a similar sense restricted westward expansion and the formation of new, interior colonies had, it is true, never been executed with complete rigidity, but they, and the uncertainties of the months preceding the war, had certainly checked many a project of large colonization and many a plan for speculation in land. Now these checks were removed. Moreover, all the vast domains of the Crown fell into the hands of the states, and were at the disposal of the state legislatures, and it was certain that these popular assemblies would dispose of them in some manner that would be agreeable to popular desires. Whether the land law in respect to old holdings should be altered by the Revolution or should remain unchanged, it was certain that in respect to new lands, on which the future hopes of American agriculture and settlement rested, a more democratic system would be installed.

Then there was the matter of the quit-rents, which in most of the colonies, according to the terms on which lands were granted to individual occupants, were to be paid to the crown or to the proprietary of the province. They ranged from a penny an acre to a shilling a hundred acres per annum. It is true that payment was largely evaded, but since the amount received at the time when the Revolution broke out was nearly $100,-000, we may count the quit-rent as something of a limitation upon the ready acquisition of land. So at any rate the colonists regarded it, for in making their new constitutions and regulations respecting lands they abolished quit-rents with great emphasis and vigor, and forbade them for the future.

Another encumbrance on land-tenure which the Revolution removed was the provision, by British statute intended to ensure an adequate supply of masts for the royal navy, that no man should cut white-pine trees on his land till the king's surveyor of woods had surveyed it and designated the trees, sometimes many in number, which were to be reserved for the king's use. It is true that the law was not rigorously enforced; it could not be, with such staff as the surveyors had. But John

Wentworth, the last royal governor of New Hampshire and the last surveyor of the king's woods in New England, tried diligently to enforce it, and, though he did it tactfully, he found it everywhere exceedingly unpopular. With the coming of the Revolution, the restriction came to an end, and fee simple was fee simple.

In the fourth place, great confiscations of Tory estates were carried out by the state legislatures, generally in the height of the war. New Hampshire confiscated twenty-eight estates, including the large property of its governor, Sir John Wentworth. In Massachusetts a sweeping act confiscated at one blow all the property of all who had fought against the United States or had even retired into places under British authority without permission from the American government. Among the lands confiscated by special mention were those of Sir William Pepperrell, the second baronet of that name, whose vast estate in Maine extended so far along the coast that it was said he could ride all the way from Kittery Point to Saco, a distance of thirty miles, on his own land. In New York, all lands and rents of the crown and all estates of fifty-nine named persons were confiscated, the greatest among them, probably, being that of the Phillipse connection. Probably something like three hundred square miles of the old Phillipse estates were confiscated, bearing a value of several hundred thousand dollars. By 1782 the state of New York had confiscated royalist property in land valued at $2,500,-000 in hard money. In all, the state probably received $3,150,000 Spanish dollars for forfeited real estate.

The largest estate confiscated was that of the Penn family, proprietaries of Pennsylvania, which they estimated at nearly a million pounds sterling. The commissioners of the state of Maryland who sold confiscated property in that state took in more than £450,000 sterling. In Georgia the single estate of Sir James Wright was valued at $160,000. The broad lands of the sixth Lord Fairfax, the genial old man in whose service Washington had first practised as a surveyor, and those of Sir John Johnson in the Mohawk country, 50,000 acres, are other examples of Tory confiscation on the grand scale. In one colony and another, hundreds of estates were confiscated. Altogether, it is evident that a great deal of land changed hands, and that the confiscation of Tory estates contributed powerfully to break up the system of large landed properties, since the states usually sold the lands thus acquired in much smaller parcels. Thus the New York law discouraged the sale of such lands in parcels of more than 500 acres. James De Lancey's real estate went to 275 persons, Roger Morris's to 250. A general idea of the extent of the confiscation may be gained from the fact that the British Parliament, after every effort to reduce the claims of the Loyalists, finally compensated them with grants aggregating over three million pounds sterling. To be sure, this was for both real and personal estate, but on the other hand it is to be said that the Loyalists themselves estimated the value of their claims upon Mr. Pitt's government as high as eight million pounds.

These Tory confiscation acts, by the way, had one curious effect upon the development of American institutions. There is no American institution more famous, none that has excited more comment in other countries, largely erroneous comment, to be sure, than the power of American courts to set aside laws for want of conformity to the Constitution. It is often spoken of as a peculiar power of the United States Supreme Court and as a peculiar invention of those who made the Constitution of 1787. In reality it is a power or duty of any court acting under a written constitution, and it was exercised in several instances by state courts before there was a Supreme Court of the United States and before the Constitution of 1787 was framed. It so happens that in most of these cases the law against which this objection was raised was a law regarding Tories. The legislatures were so hot against the Tories and so eager in the pursuit of their spoils that they quite overstepped constitutional bounds in their enactments against them. Among the lawyers there grew up the idea, virtually a new idea, that courts might set aside laws if they conflicted with the constitution of the state. The fact is, I suppose, that during this period the legislatures were in the hands of the radical revolutionaries, or extreme Whigs, while the lawyers and judges were more moderate and conservative members of that party.

But to return to the laws dealing with land alone. If, as I have suggested, nothing was more important in the American social system than its relation to the land, and if the Revolution had any social effects at all, we should expect to see it overthrowing any old-fashioned features which still continued to exist in the land laws. What, then, was the old land-law in the American colonies? The feudal ages had discovered that, if men desired to give stability to society by keeping property in the hands of the same families generation after generation, the best way to do this was to entail the lands strictly, so that the holder could not sell them or even give them away, and to have a law of primogeniture, which, in case the father made no will, would turn over all his lands to the eldest son, to the exclusion of all the other children. There could not be two better devices for forming and maintaining a land-holding aristocracy. When the Revolution broke out, Pennsylvania and Maryland had abolished primogeniture, and South Carolina had abolished entails. But in New York, New Jersey, Virginia, North Carolina, and Georgia, entails and primogeniture flourished almost as they did in old England. Indeed, Virginian entails were stricter than the English. The New England colonies had a peculiar rule of their own for the descent of land in case a man left no will. They liked a democratic distribution, and yet they could not feel quite comfortable to cut away entirely from the old English notions about the eldest son. Moreover, their Puritanical feeling for the law of Moses (Deut. xxi. 17) was very strong. Accordingly, they arranged that in such a case all the children should inherit equally, except that the eldest son should have a double share. Then came the Revolution. In ten years from the Declaration of Independence every state had abolished entails excepting two, and those were two in which entails were rare. In fifteen years every state, without exception, abolished primogeniture and in some form provided for equality of inheritance, since which time the American eldest son has never been a privileged character. It is painful to have to confess that two states, North Carolina and New Jersey, did not at once put the daughters of the Revolution upon a level with the sons. North Carolina for a few years provided for equal distribution of the lands among the sons alone, and not among daughters save in case there were no sons. New Jersey gave the sons a double share. But elsewhere absolute equality was introduced. Now I submit that this was not an accident. How hard Washington found it to get these thirteen legislatures to act together! And yet here we find them all with one accord making precisely the same changes in their land-laws. Such uniformity must have had a common cause, and where shall we find it if we do not admit that our Revolution, however much it differed from the French Revolution in spirit, yet carried in itself the seeds of a social revolution? Democratic land-tenure was the natural thing in a new country like America, and made its way at once when political revolution loosened the ties of old habit.

It seems impossible to form any secure judgment as to the total amount of land set free, or brought into a more democratic form of landholding, by all this state legislation, but there can be no question that the change was of large extent, and had extensive social consequences. In the largest of the colonies, it is estimated by the highest authority that Mr. Jefferson's act of 1776 released from entail at least half, and possibly three-quarters, of the entire "seated" area of Virginia. An act of 1705 had forbidden the docking of entails by fine and common recovery. Thenceforward an act of the legislature was necessary in order to release an estate from entail, and the pages of Hening, from that time to the Revolution, show many such enactments. But those acts seldom operated permanently to release from the practice of entail the lands to which they applied, for the new purchaser usually created a new estate tail. Moreover, the prosperous eighteenth century planter, living on an old estate in the tidewater region but ever acquiring new lands in the back country, most commonly entailed his acquired lands upon his younger sons, while passing on his inherited estate, under an old entail, to the eldest.

Social democracy and political democracy progressed together in the legislation of the Revolutionary period respecting the suffrage, for before the Revolution the electoral franchise was largely based on land. In the colonial times the right to vote had nowhere been very narrowly restricted, but in all the colonies there had been a property qualification, usually amounting to $150 or $250. In six of the colonies it had been necessary to own real estate, no amount of personal property sufficing. In the northern colonies the real estate usually fixed upon was a freehold that would rent for forty shillings—that old forty-shilling freehold which for three centuries and a half had been the standing qualification for county voters in old England. In a country so wholly given up to agriculture a real-estate qualification excluded few men. In the southern colonies, it was more usual to specify a number of acres, generally fifty. The Virginian law required fifty acres of unoccupied land, or a lot of twenty-five acres with a house upon it, or a town-lot with a house upon it. But what constituted a house? If anyone thinks that our ancestors were innocent of election dodges, he may be interested in the record of one old Virginian election, that of 1762. It appears from the journals of the House of Burgesses that William Skinner had half a lot in Elizabeth City County. On the Saturday before the election he bought a small tight-framed house, ten feet by eight, and had it moved onto the land, with the acknowledged design of thereby qualifying himself to vote, and was to pay for it later. The House allowed his vote. Thomas Payne, being owner of part of a lot, says the testimony in the journal, "purchased of one Mary Almond, for the value of 10s. a small House, about 4 and a Half Feet Pitch, 4 or 5 Feet long, and 2 or 2 and a Half Feet wide, floored or laid with Plank in the Midst of its Height, to put Milkpans, or such Things, on, and that he had the same removed in a Cart, with one Horse, with the Assistance of 7 or 8 Men, and placed on his said Lot, on purpose (as he acknowledges) to qualify himself to vote at that Election." Apparently this was going a little *too* far, and the House ruled his vote out. It then passed a law requiring that the house which was to qualify the voter must be at least twelve feet square, which certainly seems moderate enough.

The Revolution greatly altered these old colonial laws respecting the franchise. Four states, it is true, made no change in their rules, but in all the rest the freehold system was broken down. In New York the value of the freehold required was reduced, and persons who merely rented land or houses were put on a par with those who owned them. In most states, any tax-payer was now allowed to vote, whether he paid taxes on real or on personal estate. In others the amount of money required was lowered. And so it came to pass, by what was primarily a political change, but one that carried the seeds of social changes, that "We the people of the United States" who gave consent to the establishing of the Constitution was a much larger and more democratic body than "We the people of the United States" who acquiesced in the Declaration of Independence, though universal suffrage was yet a long way off.

It has been indicated already with what extensive confiscations of land the course of the Revolution had been marked. Great areas thus fell into the hands of the state governments, and most of them also possessed considerable tracts of wild lands of their own. The use made of such possessions was often such as to promote the advance of agricultural democracy. It is well known that the states were often at their wits' ends for money with which to pay their troops. In such straits an obvious resource in the case of states having a large amount of wild lands was to assign portions of them to their soldiers in lieu of pay. This was done to a very large extent, and the result was that, upon the close of the war, there set in an era of unexampled speculation in American wild lands. Soldiers sold their assignments, and the states made large sales directly, in order to pay their debts. Hence the speculation. The Duke of LaRochefoucauld-Liancourt, an émigré French nobleman who travelled extensively in the United States soon after the Revolution, tells of land near Lancaster, Pennsylvania, bought for $25 an acre, for which $100 was refused five years later. In another passage he speaks of a thousand acres near Canandaigua, New York, bought three years before at a shilling an acre, of which a half had since been sold off at prices ranging from a dollar to three dollars, and even, in some cases, twenty-five dollars. An example of one of the large sales will show, however, how low the prices would sometimes run at the great auctions, especially in the case of lands not situated near any navigable river and hence, under the conditions of transportation then prevailing, not near a market. I choose the example from the narrative of his travels printed by Henry Wansey, a Wiltshire clothier. "Monday. I attended a sale (by auction at the Tontine Coffee House) of some military lands," that is, lands given to the soldiers, "situated in the north part of New York State. Twenty-five acres in the township of Cato," he continues, "were sold at two shillings and eightpence currency" (that is, New York shillings) "per acre; . . . five hundred in Pompey at five shillings and one penny; nine hundred in Tully and Hannibal at three and eightpence; fourteen hundred in Hector and Dryden, at three and eightpence." It will be seen that the classical names which in lavish profusion decorate the map of Cortland and Onondaga counties were already there in 1789—Pompey and Tully, and Fabius and Manlius, and Cincinnatus and Marathon. It has been usual to bestow the credit or discredit of this nomenclature upon General Simeon DeWitt, the surveyor-general of the state. But the late Professor Moses Coit Tyler deemed he had proof that the dreadful deed was done by an office-boy fresh from the study of Lemprière's *Classical Dictionary*, and that the good general must be acquitted of all blame in the matter but that of leaving the selection of names to the unchastened imagination of an office-boy. However this may be, the lands sold none the less readily, 5,500,000 acres being sold by New York in a single year; and in the end, whatever allowance may be made for speculation, passed ultimately, for the most part, into the hands of small holders.

If the states, impoverished by the war and burdened with debt, found so valuable a resource through sales of state lands, we may well believe that they valued every bit of territory to which they could lay claim. Hence arose a multitude of boundary disputes, opening into several amusing but unedifying quarrels, and fostering discord between states which at that time were none too well disposed toward mutual agreement. Massachusetts found opportunity for quarrel on its western boundary

with New York. Pennsylvania and Virginia differed as
to the region where Pennsylvania now touches West
Virginia. Virginia and North Carolina differed as to
their boundary line. South Carolina and Georgia quar-
relled about their boundaries at the upper part of the
Savannah River, New York and New Hampshire about
Vermont, Connecticut and Pennsylvania about the
Wyoming country. Far more important than all these
disputes was that which raged over the control of the
western lands. The political history of this momentous
conflict, and of its happy settlement by cessions to the
Confederation, is in all the books; but the social consequences of that settlement were surely greater than
any others that have been touched upon in this lecture.

In the old states, population moved more and more
largely into the uplands in the western part of the state
—an intermediate stage toward the trans-Allegheny
migration. We may easily imagine that, on the average
in the general course of the great westward movement,
the typical family stayed a generation or two in that
region of broken or mountainous country, a hundred or
two hundred miles broad, that intervenes between the
plains of the tidewater region and the levels of the Ohio
and Mississippi valleys. It does not seem to me fantastic
to imagine that that period of sojourn of families in the
broken uplands did much to fasten the regime of small
landholding on the United States. Ohio and Indiana and
Kentucky were perhaps as capable physically of organization into great estates as Virginia or Carolina, but by
the time the swarms of settlers debouched upon those
great western plains the habit of the small farm was in
the main already fixed, and the United States was to be
a land of "peasant proprietors."

By the year 1789 the regions west of the mountains sustained already a considerable population. One of the most noteworthy features of American social history in the period immediately succeeding the Revolution is the prodigiously rapid migration of settlers into the new West. The movement had not waited for the Revolution to reach its slow conclusion. But in 1783, when the news of peace came to America, the stream of westward migration assumed proportions unknown before. Kentucky was erected into a district, with regular courts. Trade by way of the Ohio began. Schools were started. To the meeting-houses already built by the Baptists and Dutch Reformed was added a log church for the Presbyterians. A race-track was laid out; and Kentucky entered upon the second stage of her existence. The settlements in what is now Tennessee prospered similarly. In 1783 there were probably twenty-five thousand inhabitants in the settlements west of the Alleghenies. The number increased more rapidly in Kentucky than elsewhere. Virginia gave lands in that region to the soldiers of her disbanded forces in commutation of their claims for pay and bounty, and thus it came about that Kentucky contained in after years an unusually large number of men who had been soldiers of the Revolution —sturdy progenitors for an infant state. Since the war had impoverished many of the planters of the tidewater regions of Virginia and neighboring states, many of these now sought to repair their fortunes by a new venture, and migrated beyond the mountains with what property they had, to begin life anew on virgin soil. Thousands of migrants poured into Kentucky in the long caravans that made their difficult way over the mountains by the Wilderness Road. Even larger num-

bers floated down the Ohio to the shores of Kentucky or
the newer acquisitions on the northern bank of the river,
the Illinois country, now more commonly called the
Northwest Territory. An eye-witness, writing from Kentucky in December 1785, states that, in the thirty-nine
days preceding, thirty-nine boats, with an average of
ten persons upon each, had passed down the Ohio River
to the Falls. The stream of migration increased each
year. In the last half of the year 1787 a hundred and
forty-six boats passed by Fort Harmar, conveying 3,196
persons, 1,371 horses, 165 wagons, and cattle and sheep
in proportion. In the year ending in November 1788, a
letter from that fort assures us, 967 boats had passed
down, carrying 18,370 persons, with 7,986 horses, and
with wagons and cattle and sheep. The population of
Kentucky, which in 1785 was estimated at from twenty
to thirty thousand, is stated in the census of 1790 to
have been 74,000, while 37,000 more dwelt in the settlements to the southward of Kentucky, and a few thousands in the Northwest Territory, where systematic
colonization had just been begun by the Ohio Company.
With each succeeding census the number rose with
wonderful rapidity.

The movement of westward expansion which thus
began is one of the most familiar facts of American history. But perhaps we do not always remember how
peculiar it is, nor take notice of all its consequences. Is
there any other great country whose center of population moves over the country many miles each decade, as
does ours, which in a hundred and thirty years moved
westward from the Chesapeake to Illinois? But what are
the social results? A nation's center of population is, in
a way, its center of gravity. A shifting center of gravity

forces a nation into a perpetual readjustment of its life. That which was the center of the merchant's particular branch of business ten years ago is no longer its center now; the farmer, the commercial traveller, the engineer, the speculator, must learn anew, every ten years, the social geography of his country. Restless change, unceasing adaptation to new conditions, will be the characteristic of such a nation. Its members will be distinguished from those of other nations by a superior versatility, a quickness of adaptation, a readiness toward new undertakings and an openness to new ideas, such as can be bred only by past habits of perpetual readjustment and renovation.

Not less noteworthy was the influence of the western region in promoting that growth of political and social democracy which was one of the most precious legacies of the Revolutionary period. The dweller upon the broad prairies, though individual and sometimes intractable, was likely to be expansive and genial. His wide horizon was hostile to narrow views. The influx into any given area of men of all sorts and from all parts of the world tended to break up the distinctions which in more settled societies distinguished man from man. And so a hearty belief in human equality was likely to be a part of the generous creed of the West. Moreover, the very conditions of life, the intense struggle for existence which every individual had usually to go through, tended of themselves to equalize men and to draw them together in the bonds of mutual sympathy. The process, therefore, which had marked the Atlantic settlements in comparison with the countries of Europe, was likely to mark the West even more than the East, and to push forward still more the development of American democracy.

III. *Industry and Commerce*

P ROBABLY the World War has cured us all of the
habit of supposing that a war absorbs completely
the energies of a nation. So great is the stress and
excitement which wars have produced, that it has been
easy to imagine that, in past history, everyone has been
fully occupied with them; but even in this recent instance, when war affected a greater percentage of each
nation than usual, this was far from being the case. It
never happens in a civilized country that even half the
men of military age are in the army when the country is
engaged in war. In our Civil War, the number of men
between eighteen and sixty in the Union states was
about five million and a half when the war broke out,
but the largest number of troops in the army at any one
time, including regulars, militia, and volunteers, was
never much above one million, less than one-fifth. In
the Confederate states, whose energies were more completely absorbed in the struggle, the army, at its largest
extent, included a number equal to nearly a third of the
white male population between the ages mentioned. It
is plain then that, however intensely a nation may be
interested in a war, the larger number of its citizens remain nevertheless occupied in other than military pursuits. They labor on the farm, in mines and factories and
workshops, in their wonted vocations, in order to support themselves and to produce the wealth necessary
for the maintenance of warfare. Especially is this true
in a long and dragging war. Modern warfare costs so

much that it is expedient that quick work be made of it, and therefore that as many men as possible be diverted from their ordinary industrial employments and put into the field or into munition-making. The industrial recuperation of the country is a matter to which they can give their attention later. But in previous centuries wars went more slowly, and it was necessary that many men should remain at their homes and continue the ordinary work of industrial production. King Alfred, it will be remembered, divided his West-Saxon army into two equal divisions, that one might remain in the field while the other attended to the labors of their rude agriculture.

At the time when the Revolutionary war broke out, the population of the thirteen colonies amounted to about two and a half million men, women, and children. The number of men of fighting age, say from eighteen to sixty, would then be something like seven hundred thousand. A much smaller proportion of them was in the fighting force of General Washington than that which the United States of 1865 yielded to the army of General Grant. In 1776, when the army was at its largest, it numbered, including both Continentals and state militia, not quite ninety thousand men, about one-eighth of the men of fighting age. In the years 1779 and 1780 it was but half as large, not more than a sixteenth part of the male inhabitants of military age. And, of the seven years of the war, more were like 1779 and 1780 than like 1776.

The thought need only be suggested, how widespread an apathy is evidenced by these figures, even after we have made allowance for the thousands of brave sailors who were fighting the battles of the Revolution in naval vessels and privateers. The figures are mentioned rather to show that, ardently as many thousands were engaged in the actual work of fighting, for most men in the thirteen American states industrial life went on during these seven years, not without disturbance, to be sure, but without cessation in its development. It may be profitable to turn aside from the stirring records of military achievement, to see what was being done in agriculture, in manufactures, and in commerce during the same period, and how far and in what ways, if at all, their development was affected by the war and the political revolution.

It was remarked in the preceding lecture that vastly the greater number of the people of the American colonies were occupied with agriculture. It will therefore be proper to begin with this industry though it was affected less by the Revolution than some other classes of occupation. One very important series of effects has been touched upon in the last lecture, the freeing of the soil from all connection with the feudal land-law, the breaking-up of large estates, the universal extension, in the North at least, of that system of small or moderate farms, cultivated by the owner's own hands, which so long remained the characteristic mark of the agricultural system of America.

Throughout the colonial period, American agriculture was still in a stage of experimentation, as was natural in a new country to which farmers came from an old country. Farmers had tested the suitableness of the American soil and climate to the agricultural products of Europe so thoroughly that hardly a single important species of domestic animal and hardly a single important species of cultivated plant originating in Europe, has, it is said, been introduced since the Revolutionary

War. But American agriculture had been careless and wasteful. Land was so cheap and labor so much scarcer than in Europe that it did not pay to apply to American soil the careful intensive cultivation of England and France. The result was that, in the times just preceding the Revolution, colonial agriculture was in a poor condition. The fields had been worn out by hasty methods, and better methods were not learned because, with all the experimenting that had gone on, the results of experience were not diffused among farmers, for lack of agricultural societies and periodicals.

Meanwhile, during the middle portion of the eighteenth century, the agriculture of England and France had been undergoing improvements so great as almost to constitute a revolution in methods. But little of this revival found its way to America, and that mainly through the efforts of one man, and he a clergyman. The Rev. Jared Eliot, grandson of the apostle John Eliot, was for nearly half a century pastor of the church at Killingworth, Connecticut. He was a member of the Royal Society in London, and as a physician in difficult cases had so great repute that he was even called to Newport and Boston for such purposes. This man, after travels in Europe extending even as far as Russia, brought home the knowledge of good methods of agriculture, wrote and published essays, tried experiments on his Connecticut farm, introduced clover-sowing for the recuperation of worn-out fields, and was in many ways useful in his day and generation. But in general the better modes of cultivation which Europe had lately been learning were but little known in the American colonies when the war began. In particular, the domestic animals of America were, on account of the inferiority of the native American grasses, much smaller and poorer than those of Europe. Indeed, the opinion prevailed in Europe that all animated nature degenerated on the western continent, and the chief of naturalists, Buffon, set forth this view in his writings, until Jefferson, to confute him, sent to America for the skeleton of an elk.

But the Revolution brought American farmers into more intimate association with Europeans, and especially with Frenchmen, and thus gave them a chance to learn more of the recent agricultural improvements. Their minds were widened by the war. Best of all, the organizing habit which was bred in the American mind by this period of political and social reorganization gave an impetus to the much-needed formation of agricultural societies. These had been in Europe the most important means of disseminating information regarding improved methods or the results of experiment, and of awakening the minds of farmers. In Scotland the "Society of Improvers in the Knowledge of Agriculture" had been formed in 1723, and others had followed during the next decades. Agriculture, which had been practically stationary from the times of the Roman Empire, began to awaken from its long sleep. Now, as soon as the Revolution was over, societies of similar purpose began to be formed in America. The first such in the United States was the "Society for the Promotion of Agriculture" founded at Charleston, South Carolina, in August 1785. The Philadelphia society of the same name was founded later in the same year, that of New York in 1791, those of Massachusetts and Connecticut in 1792.

These societies began a most valuable work of experiment, comparison, and diffusion of information. The cast-iron plough began to be introduced. The cradle began to supplant the sickle. Efforts were made to improve livestock, in spite of the severe laws which forbade under heavy penalties the exportation of southdowns from England or merinos from Spain. And farming, as it grew more skilful, grew more profitable. The English economist, Dr. Thomas Cooper, in his book of information for persons intending to emigrate to the United States, advises the man of middling fortune to become a farmer there. (He adds, among his items of minor advice, that the intending emigrant had better take flower-seeds with him, since the Americans care so much more for utility than for ornament that flower-seeds are hard to procure in the States.)

American manufactures were much more directly and conspicuously affected by the Revolution than American agriculture. In the first place, the Revolution did away at once with all those annoying restrictions with which the English Parliament had endeavored to burden colonial manufactures. In the long list of American grievances against the British government, not the least had been the series of petty enactments by which it had been sought to confine the colonies to the production of raw materials, while England monopolized the manufacturing industries of both countries. So early as 1699 the woollen manufactures of New England had become large enough to attract the attention of old England. An act was passed in that year to prevent, under heavy penalties, the export from the colonies, or from colony to colony, of any "Wool, Woolfells, Shortlings, Morlings, Wool Flocks, Worsted, Bay or Woollen Yarn, Cloath,

Serge, Bays, Kerseys, Says, Frizes, Druggets, Cloath Serges, Shalloons or any other Drapery, Stuffs or Woollen Manufactures whatsoever." In 1719 the House of Commons resolved "that the erection of manufactories in the colonies tends to lessen their dependence on Great Britain." The plentiful supply of beaver in the colonies led to a considerable manufacture of hats. In 1732 an act of Parliament was passed which forbade the exportation of hats from the colonies, and prohibited any hatter from taking more than two apprentices. The iron manufacture grew. England welcomed the increased supply of pig and bar iron, but wished absolutely to engross to herself all further manufactures. In 1750 Parliament prohibited the erection of any rolling-, slitting-, or plating-mill, and all manufacture of steel. In this, as in so many other ways, the Revolution enfranchised America. American manufactures might henceforth be developed solely in accordance with American interests.

Again, the non-importation agreements and the war which speedily ensued cut off at once nearly all of the stream of goods hitherto imported from England. The colonists were thrown back upon their own resources. For eight years they were obliged, for the most part, either to get along without these goods, which in some cases was very difficult, or to provide them for themselves. American ingenuity, already developed by the various needs of a pioneer civilization, was set to work to devise, as well as it could, the means of supplying its own wants independently of England or Europe.

Even before the passage of the Stamp Act such results were foreshadowed. A letter from a Virginian to a correspondent in Bristol, England, written in the autumn of 1764, says: "The Acts of Parliament have made such impressions on the minds of the northward people and the men-of-war so strictly enforce them, that there is an entire stagnation of trade. Nothing do they talk of but their own manufactures. The downfall of England and the rise of America is sung by the common ballad-singers about the streets, as if in a little time we should supply ourselves with most of the necessaries we used before to take from England."

At New York there was immediately formed a "Society for the Promotion of Arts, Agriculture, and Economy." Great efforts were made to foster the manufacture of linens and woollens. Large numbers of people agreed to abstain from the use of mourning at funerals, such as black cloth, scarfs, gloves, and rings, not of domestic manufacture, and a useful simplification of funerals resulted. To keep up the supply of material for woollen manufactures, most of the inhabitants agreed not to eat any lamb or mutton, and not to deal with any butcher who should kill any lambs.

This movement was so extensive as to produce a genuine effect of alarm among the merchants in Great Britain. When Townshend, in 1767, proposed his duties on paper, glass, painters' colors, and tea, the enthusiasm for domestic manufactures revived. Resolutions were made to abstain from the use of "loaf sugar, . . . coaches and carriages of all sorts, imported hats and clothing, . . . gold, silver, and thread lace, gold and silver buttons," plate, diamonds, clocks, watches, jewelry, muffs, furs, millinery, starch, women's and children's stays, velvet, gauze, silks, and many other articles more difficult to do without. The spinning-wheel came into renewed use in every household, and homespun was worn by the wealthiest. Spinning matches at neighbors' houses became a common occurrence, and an excellent outlet for patriotic ardor. Imports from England into the northern colonies went down in 1769 to not much more than a third of what they were in 1768. Hence the repeal of all the taxes save that on tea. At Harvard Commencement, in 1770, the graduating class appeared in black cloth entirely of American manufacture.

The Virginia Convention of August 1774 resolved that attention should be turned "from the cultivation of tobacco to the cultivation of such articles as may form a basis for domestic manufactures, which we will endeavor to encourage throughout this Colony to the utmost of our abilities." The first Continental Congress recommended to all the colonies the encouragement of manufactures. The colonies offered bounties and prizes, and encouraged the formation of societies of arts. In 1775 the "United Company of Philadelphia for promoting American Manufactures" was formed, to organize on a large scale the making of American woollen, linen, and cotton cloth. It continued, with varying fortunes, and supplied a part of the cloth for the Revolutionary army. A great part of the privations which that army suffered arose from the undeveloped state of the manufacturing industries of the country. Woollen materials were hardly to be had for love or money, and the soldiers often shivered through a campaign in clothing chiefly consisting of linen. At Baltimore, we are told, General Lafayette was invited to a ball. He went, but did not dance. Instead, he addressed the ladies: "You are very handsome, you dance very prettily, your ball is very fine—but my soldiers have no shirts." They ran home and went to work, and in a few days the product of their energy and industry was placed at the service of the marquis.

The intense demand for woollen goods reacted upon the manufacture of machinery for making them. Great attention was given in several states to the devising of new processes for making wool-cards. Indeed, the Revolution brought out in strong relief the inventiveness of the American, a trait for which he is now so famous, and which a century and a half of life in a new country had powerfully developed in private, but which now came forward prominently into public notice. Patents and bounties began to be granted by governments, and there began to be famous inventors, like Oliver Evans and Amos Whittemore, in the place of the inglorious genius, farmer or farm-hand, who could make anything with a jack-knife, but whose fame did not extend beyond his village.

It was natural that in the development of certain classes of manufacture the Revolution should have a peculiar importance. There were arms and munitions of war to be provided, for instance. Great Britain in 1774 forbade the exportation of fire-arms, gun-powder, and other military stores. Some manufacture of them had already begun in the colonies. But now Congress and the state Committees of Safety took hold of the matter as a thing of vital importance in the struggle. For the making of gunpowder, saltpeter was collected from old cellars and stables. As for arms, though the Americans had not made them in great numbers, they had become very skilful in the art, as was natural in a nation so full of hunters. Governor Richard Penn, in his examination before the House of Lords just as the war was beginning, stated, in reply to the inquiries of the Duke of Rich-

mond, that the casting of iron and brass cannon at
Philadelphia had been carried to great perfection, and
that the workmanship and finish of the small arms was
all that could be desired. Rifles were made in the colonies at that time which were thought as good as any
that were imported. Gunsmiths were numerous. But in
this, as in other trades, there was little organization.
Each gunsmith worked for himself, or perhaps had two
or three men to help him, so that the committees of
Congress had to make their contracts for small quantities, and place them here and there with individuals,
and, after all, to get most of their arms from Europe.

In 1778 the government armory at Springfield was
established, where the works would be remote from the
incursions of the enemy. For a similar reason, much
gun-making was carried on in Maryland. To stimulate
the manufacture of such things, Congress called upon
the states to exempt from taxation all who were engaged
in them. That they were sometimes at the greatest
straits for material, may well be imagined, when all the
ordinary channels of trade were closed or perverted. We
hear of one foundry idle for a long time from sheer want
of copper. A few days before the battle of Brandywine,
messengers were sent to the mills of the Dunkers or
German "Brethren" at Ephrata for a supply of paper
for cartridges. The mill's products happened to be ex-
hausted, so far as clean paper was concerned. But the
fraternity also did a printing business, and had on hand
an edition of Fox's *Book of Martyrs*, in sheets, then
ready for the bindery. They generously placed this mass
of printed paper at the service of their country, and in
the ensuing battle the good old martyrologist, in the

form of cartridges, went up in smoke and flames for the good cause, like the martyrs of whom he wrote.

Paper-mills increased enormously during the Revolutionary period. One important reason for this was the great increase of newspapers. There were thirty-seven in 1776. In 1789 there were probably over a hundred. The addiction of the American to this sort of reading was already remarkable. "All these people," says the Duke of LaRochefoucauld of the people of the house at which he was stopping in Marlborough, Massachusetts, "busy themselves much with politics, and from the landlord down to the housemaid they all read two newspapers a day."

It will perhaps hardly be imagined that, of the manufactures which the Revolution directly affected, one of those most highly stimulated was that of salt. Before the Revolution, the saline deposits of central New York and of the remoter interior had not yet been reached, and salt was almost altogether procured from abroad. It was an article of prime importance to the Americans, partly because of the great amounts used in the fisheries, partly because it was much given to cattle, and largely also because our fathers made so enormous use of salted provisions and exported so many barrels of them. The chief supply of salt had been obtained by the ships which went out with lumber, fish and other provisions, and tobacco. When they came back, they often brought coarse salt as ballast, from the ports of southern Europe, the Canary or Madeira or West Indian Islands.

The interruption of this trade produced a distressing scarcity of salt. It rose to six dollars a bushel. Many attempts were made, all along the shore of the Atlantic, to procure salt by boiling sea-water in kettles. Finally, an enterprising sailor residing upon Cape Cod conceived the idea of making salt more economically, after the manner followed in the Mediterranean, by evaporation by the sun's heat acting on sea-water in large and shallow vats. Soon many such went into operation, and the wind-mills by which the salt water was pumped up became a noteworthy feature of the not-too-varied scenery of the Cape. This particular manufacture, being of necessity carried on in positions near the sea, was more than ordinarily exposed to the destructive attacks of the British. But it developed in the United States a considerable industry.

On the other hand, the war destroyed for the time that which had been before the war the chief of American manufactures for exportation, namely, shipbuilding. Writers in that time and since have been fond of declaiming against the oppressiveness of the Navigation Acts. Their burden was in many ways difficult to bear—or would have been had they not been so systematically and successfully evaded by the enterprising colonists. But it is certain that they fostered American shipbuilding in the highest degree. In the years 1769, 1770, and 1771, nearly four hundred vessels a year, large and small, were built in the colonies. When the war broke out, 400,000 tons of colonial-built shipping were employed in the general commerce of Great Britain. The severing of the political connection with England deprived American shipwrights of this advantage, and for a time their trade languished, but after the peace it recovered with surprising swiftness.

It is not possible to dwell upon all the varieties of manufacture which the Revolution called into existence or stimulated in America, though it would be pleasant to speak of the development of the piano-forte, whose prodigious frequency in all subsequent times might easily deceive unwary travellers into the belief that we were a musical people. The leading manufactures when the war ended, suffice it to say, were, beside those that have been mentioned, those from iron and leather, and that of glass. Europeans believed that, when the artificial stimulus produced by the war was withdrawn, many of these would not continue to succeed. Dr. Cooper, an intelligent and fair-minded man, thought it would be a long time before manufactures of woollen, linen, and cotton goods, or of pottery, would succeed. Wages were too high. "I have no doubt, however," he says, "of the success of a glass manufacture, a gunpowder manufacture, of a paper maker, a paper stainer, a letter founder, a manufactory of all the heavy kinds of iron-work, such as castings from the ore, pig iron, bar iron, rolling mills, slitting mills, and the making of nails." Of most of these there were already examples in the country by the year 1789. To illustrate the increase of mills of various sorts, the Duke of LaRochefoucauld says that, ten years after the Revolution, Brandywine Creek, in the seven or eight miles of its short course through Delaware, turned about sixty mills.

But it should be understood that but a small part of the manufacturing enterprise which the Revolution evoked expended itself in manufacturing establishments. The bulk of American manufacturing was after all domestic. In most parts of the country by far the greatest part of the clothing was made in the household. When Tench Coxe investigated this subject, a few years later, he said that typical neighborhoods of twenty families rich and poor, in Virginia, showed in one case domestic manufactures of the value of $1670 in one year, in the other of $1791. For another evidence of their extent, we know that there were forty-one fulling-mills in New Jersey at a time when there were in that state no established manufactories of cloth, none, that is, other than the domestic; also, that one shop in Philadelphia, a few years after the Revolution, sold in one year fifteen hundred sets of spinning-wheel irons.

This domestic mode was often employed in trades to which we should hardly think of its being applicable now. Take for instance, the manufacture of nails. It was one of those branches in which the country earliest became independent of British supplies, and one of those in which the effects of the war were first felt among British manufacturers—at least so said Lord Dudley in the House of Peers in 1776. Yet it was in very large part, if not chiefly, a domestic manufacture. In one of the first debates in the House of Representatives, Fisher Ames of Massachusetts said: "This manufacture, with very little encouragement, has grown up very remarkably. It has become common for the country people in Massachusetts to erect small forges in their chimney corners, and in winter, and on evenings when little other work can be done, great quantities of nails are made, even by children. These people take the rod-iron of the merchant and return him the nails, and in consequence of this easy mode of barter, the manufacture is prodigiously great." This bit may serve to show us that, if it seems a long distance from these humble beginnings to the vast industrial development of today, nevertheless the industry and grit were already present which were in time to make this the greatest manufacturing country of the world.

If we turn now to the consideration of internal trade, it is easy to see that here the war could do little but harm to the industrial life of the country. A comparatively poor country, being compelled to manage an expensive war, of necessity had recourse to large issues of paper money. Millions upon millions were sent forth. Each one of the thirteen states issued notes which competed for circulation with those of the Continental Congress. In December 1778, the Continental bills, then considerably exceeding a hundred millions in amount, had depreciated until they were worth only a twentieth part of their face value. Yet Congress maintained the certainty of their redemption, and resolved "that any contrary report was false, and derogatory to its honor." In August 1779, a paper dollar was worth only three or four cents in silver. In December it was worth less than two and a half cents. "A wagon-load of money," it was said, "would scarcely purchase a wagon-load of provisions." In April 1781, Congress proposed an exchange of the old bills for new, at the rate of forty dollars for one, and the measure was received with favor, though it wiped out at one stroke thirty-nine fortieths of such debt as was represented by the paper money. A Philadelphia wag made a blanket for his dog out of the Continental paper, and paraded him upon the street in that array.

Under such circumstances it was hardly to be expected that trade should flourish, even in regions which did not not feel heavily the pressure of war and were not in danger from incursions or depredations of the enemy. Prices went up and up. Conventions of counties, and finally conventions at which several states were represented, met, for instance at Providence, at Springfield, at Hartford, and at Yorktown, and attempted to bolster up the failing credit of the paper money by laws declaring that the prices of commodities should not rise above certain figures enumerated upon their lists. Nevertheless prices rose. Economic laws were stronger than those of state legislatures, however resolute and patriotic. In 1781 we find quotations of shoes at twenty pounds a pair, milk at fifteen shillings a quart, potatoes at ninety shillings a bushel, rum at forty-five shillings a quart, corn at forty dollars a bushel, a cow at $1200.

The depreciation, of course, bore hardest upon men who lived upon salaries, or in other ways had fixed incomes. Dr. Ezra Ripley, who was settled over the parish of Concord, Massachusetts, in 1788, gives a vivid account of his trials in his *Half-Century Discourse* preached in 1828. He says: "With all his exertions in various ways, as teaching scholars, manual labor, etc., your pastor could not have waded through, had it not been for a particular event in Providence, and the long credit given him by one benevolent trader (Deacon John White) in town." For those whose deacons were not benevolent, as no doubt sometimes happened, there must have been many privations while the currency was in this disordered condition.

It should be remembered, also, how lacking in the colonies were the most ordinary facilities for the transaction of large business. Transportation was in an almost primitive condition. It casts a flash of light upon the provinciality of American life at the time of the Declaration of Independence, to reflect that at that time there was not a single bank in the whole country. The first organized bank in the United States, the Bank of North America, had its origin in a meeting of citizens of Philadelphia, in June 1780, to devise means of furnishing supplies to the army, then in a state of great destitution. It was then resolved to open a "security subscription to the amount of £300,000, Pennsylvania currency, real money." Robert Morris subscribed ten thousand pounds to this fund, and Tom Paine five hundred dollars. Morris made the plan for the Bank of North America, which was chartered by Congress on the last day of the year 1781. The charter permitted a capital of ten million dollars, but individuals paid in only $85,000, and the government, which subscribed $250,000, paid in only $50,000. The bank began its career with $300,000. Besides this pioneer bank, which is still in existence, only two others had come into operation in 1789, the Massachusetts Bank in Boston, and the Bank of New York.

One branch of American industrial life made great gains because of the war, to which we have not yet alluded, and that is maritime commerce. Under all the restrictions imposed by the Navigation Acts, American commerce had been constantly growing, and there were even merchant princes in some of the greater ports, or traders so esteemed in that day. The war interrupted commerce greatly, of course. It could not fail to do so, in view of the prodigious navy of Great Britain. Nevertheless it furnished the maritime development of the nation, and that in two ways, first by stimulating privateering adventure, and secondly by removing legal restrictions and opening a free course to American shipping into all parts of the world save those under British control. Privateering was of course a mode of warfare, but the impulse that led men into it was largely commercial, or at least that same love of gain which also inspired commerce.

The Americans were old hands at privateering. In the War of the Spanish Succession, in the Spanish war of 1739, the French war of 1744, and especially in the French and Indian War, the business had attained prodigious proportions. In 1745, Captain Simeon Potter, of Bristol, Rhode Island, sailing in the *Prince Charles of Lorraine*, had ravaged fifteen hundred miles of territory on the Spanish Main. In one cruise, in 1759 and 1760, Abraham Whipple of Rhode Island captured twenty-three prizes, valued at a million dollars. Now when the Revolution broke out the memory of these exploits and receipts was still fresh, and New England had many skilful seamen idle because of the serious interruption to the fisheries which had been caused by the presence of the British warships off the coast. Here was all the material for a great development of privateering enterprise.

Sometimes it is difficult to distinguish, in the maritime history of the Revolution, what was naval endeavor, carried on in government vessels, which was war, from that which was carried on in private vessels, which was half war, half business. But it seems clear that the privateering successes of the Revolution quite overshadowed those obtained by the vessels of the federal and state governments, and that they made more impression upon the enemy. Service on a privateer was more attractive to bold sailors, for it offered prospects of greater gains. So great were the profits that New England shipping interests, it is said, were never more prosperous than in the last years of the war. In 1781 Salem alone had fifty-nine vessels, carrying four thousand men. In the year preceding, the Admiralty Court of the Essex district of Massachusetts had condemned 818 prizes. In the single month of May 1779 eighteen prizes were brought into New London. In the course of the whole war more than five hundred privateers were commissioned by the various states, and probably as many as ninety thousand Americans were, first and last, engaged in these voyages, a number of men almost as great as served in the army, and greater than that of the army in any single year save one. Two-thirds of these men were from Massachusetts, the rest from the other New England states and from the Delaware river.

A good notion of the importance of the privateers' exploits may be gained from the fact that in 1776 insurance on cargoes going from the West Indies to England rose to twenty-eight per cent of the value of the ship and goods. Special types of vessels were developed for these purposes, and American designs in shipbuilding permanently benefited. "Thousands of schemes of privateering," wrote John Adams, "are afloat in American imaginations." At the end of that year, 1776, no less than two hundred and fifty West Indiamen had been captured, and the injury already done to the West India trade was estimated in England at £1,800,000. Robert Morris is said to have raised his fortune to between £300,000 and £400,000 by such ventures. Abraham Whipple, in the *Providence*, once fell in with a large convoy of English merchantmen bound from the West Indies to England. He disguised his vessel, or concealed her character, so that he boldly entered the fleet as one of their number. After dark on each of ten successive nights he boarded and captured some vessel from the convoy. Upon each of these he put a small prize crew and sent it away secretly to Boston. Eight of them reached that port, and their cargoes sold for more than a million dollars. Beside exploits in the nearer waters, the privateers sought their gain in remoter seas. Even the waters around Britain were not safe from them, and the privateer *General Mifflin* hovered around the North Cape and took seven or eight English vessels on their way to Archangel.

All this would have various effects upon the development of regular commerce. It would immensely stimulate boldness and enterprise on the part of captains and sailors. If when peace was made they could bring themselves down from these sublime heights of romantic adventure to the sober level of peaceful trade at all, it must be trade with a spice of adventure in it at least.

One of the least happy avenues through which this spirit of venture found expression was the revival of the African slave trade. In years just before the outbreak of hostilities that traffic was flourishing. During the war importations into the Continental colonies ceased almost entirely. The natural effect in the West Indies was a glut of the market. Peace was promptly followed by a great revival of the trade. Not only had the planters been deprived during seven years of the opportunity for their customary buying, but they had also lost many of their negroes by the depredations of the invading army. So rapid was the increase in importations into South Carolina that by 1785 that state was once more debating the wisdom of curtailing the traffic, at least for a time. During the course of the debate it was stated that 7000 negroes had been imported into Charleston since the peace. The assembly passed a law forbidding importations, effective in 1787. In Rhode

Island a law was passed forbidding any citizen of the state to take part in the trade. Thereafter any participation in it by Rhode Islanders was illicit and furtive.

In forms more respectable a pronounced taste for longer voyages, for trade with remoter regions, is found among seamen when the war ended. In 1783 men began to talk in Salem of the China trade. The Orient had for them something of the same charm which it had exercised upon the minds of Prince Henry the Navigator and Vasco da Gama. If the traders themselves had no gift of any but prosaic expression, who shall say, nevertheless, that there was not a poetic element in this looking toward a wider horizon for the expansive influence of the young republic?

At all events the new trade went on. In 1784 Captain John Green, in the *Empress*, sailed direct from New York to Canton. The *Grand Turk*, Captain West, made a voyage that year to the Cape of Good Hope, and in 1785 to the Isle of France and Canton. So rapidly was the trade pushed that in 1789, only four years later, a British observer reports that, of eighty-six ships in the harbor of Canton, fifteen were American. Brissot says that in that same year forty-four vessels sailed out of Boston alone for the Northwest Coast, the East Indies, and China. Many of these ships were in the command of boys under twenty-one.

The incentive to the trade was the enormous profits which might be made by these direct voyages to regions with which the colonies had traded only indirectly. The usual profit on muslins and calicoes from Calcutta was a hundred per cent. The ship *Benjamin Silsbee* took less than $1,000 worth of plain glass tumblers to the Isle of France, and sold them for $12,000. Ebenezer Parsons, a younger brother of Chief Justice Parsons, sent vessels from Gloucester to the Indies, which then carried cargoes of coffee around to Smyrna, making large profits, sometimes as much as three hundred or four hundred per cent. Everyone knows the story of Lord Timothy Dexter and his cargo of warming-pans, but that was of a later time.

But beside such effects as arose from heightened boldness and enterprise, the Revolution affected American commerce in another and very substantial way. It is familiar that, among the grievances that gave rise to the Revolution, none was more insisted upon than the Navigation Acts. These purported to confine the commerce of the colonies for the benefit of the mother country. Most colonial products could be sent abroad only to English ports. It is quite true that the laws were extensively evaded; nevertheless they did operate to some extent. Therefore the Declaration of Independence brought to American commerce a release from fetters. The commerce of the world, except with England, was thrown open to the new United States. Even before independence was declared, the Continental Congress had so far relaxed the American Association as to permit the export of produce to all countries not under British rule, and free trade in all goods not of British origin. New channels of trade were thus at once opened. Shipments of tobacco and other staples were made to France, Spain, and Holland, either directly or through the West Indian possessions of those countries, which had a great demand for American lumber, fish, and salted meat. Indirectly, it proved possible to keep up a trade, though at some risk in case of discovery, with the British West Indies also. The intermediary was St. Eustatius, a little

Dutch island of the Caribbean group, which had a good roadstead and was a free port. Here the goods of the revolted colonies of the mainland could be exchanged against those of the still loyal colonies of the West Indies, much to the advantage of both, for we are told that the cessation of the ordinary supplies from the mainland colonies had caused in Jamaica alone the starvation of fifteen thousand negroes. When Rodney captured St. Eustatius in 1781, sober authorities estimated the value of the capture at more than three million pounds sterling.

By all such means, American commerce began to recover from the first shocks and losses of war. In April 1777, a Boston merchant writes: "Though our money has depreciated, the internal strength of the Country is greater than when the war began; and there is hardly a town that has not more ratable polls than at that time. And though many individuals suffer, yet the farmer and the bulk of the people gain by the war; and Great Britain therefore ought not to think of ever getting a peace without allowing independence." That the people who surrounded him were not without the comforts and even the luxuries of life is evident from other passages in his letters. French silks, cambrics, etc., are called for. "I would observe," he says, "that people dress as much and as extravagantly as ever. The ladies lay out much on their heads, in flowers and white gauze; and hoop petticoats seem crawling in."

We must not deny that the war brought with it, as all wars do, great losses and great derangements of economic and industrial life. But, so far as commerce was concerned, it brought with it the brightest promise of

wider and richer development in the future. Not, however, in the immediate future. For, in spite of all that
has been said, one great obstacle hindered for six years
after the conclusion of peace in 1783 the best development of American trade, whether domestic or foreign.
Nothing is more necessary to the life of trade than a
strong and firm government. Now it is notorious that
the government of the United States under the Confederation was abjectly weak and uncertain. The government of the United States had no power to raise
money to pay its debts, no power to give stability to
the currency or stay the depreciation of its own promises
to pay, no power to compel the states to keep their
promises or do justice, or even to keep the peace with
each other, no power to preserve them from internal
discords and insurrections, no power to provide a uni-
form tariff law, so necessary for the successful calcula-
tions of merchants, no power to secure to foreign
creditors their just dues, no power to execute its own
treaties, no power to keep up a satisfactory consular
service, no power even to regulate port dues and light-
houses. Taxes were resisted, and all manner of economic
heresies were afloat.

Thus the newly-arisen enterprise in commerce, which
the war had called into existence, found itself hampered by the weakness of the federal organization. This
furnishes the explanation of the fact that, in all the
efforts which statesmen were making in these years
from 1783 to 1789 to erect a stronger federal government, they found their best helpers among the commercial classes. To these the necessity for a stronger
government was so apparent that it did not need argu-

ment. Hence it should not surprise us that the pathway to the creation of a firmer union led through considerations of commercial regulations. The conferences about the regulation of commerce between Maryland and Virginia, held at Alexandria and at Mount Vernon in 1785, paved the way to the Annapolis Convention, which in 1786 met to consider the policy of such regulations between a larger number of the states or, if possible, the whole union. From the Annapolis Convention of 1786 sprang the Philadelphia Convention of 1787, which framed the Constitution of the United States. And as commerce helped to bring about the better union, so the firmer union helped to forward commerce. From the time of the adoption of that constitution, American shipping entered upon an era of immense prosperity, which speedily gave unbounded fame to the merchant marine of the United States.

Upon the statue of the first William Pitt which the City of London erected in his honor in the midst of that hive of industry, they placed an inscription commemorating him as that great minister who had made trade flourish by means of war. So remarkable a commendation no statesman of our Revolution could have claimed, nor have I any desire to maintain that that war was not, like nearly every other war, accompanied by great losses and injuries to our economic system. What I have tried to show is, that American industry profited by it in the end. The Civil War of sixty years ago, which so desolated and impoverished the South, nevertheless, by sweeping away an obsolete economic and social system, set free the economic life of the South, to enter upon that career of varied and boundless prosperity of which we have seen only the beginnings. The effort of this lecture has been to show in what ways the Revolution brought ultimate benefit to the agriculture, the manufactures, and the commerce of the United States of America.

IV. *Thought and Feeling*

THE preceding lectures have concerned themselves solely with the visible or tangible effects which the American Revolution brought about in the social system of America. The imponderable effects which it may have caused in the field of public opinion or popular emotion are not so easily identified or traced. One reason for this rests upon the fundamental fact that in the order of time causes are presumed to precede effects. We cannot satisfy ourselves as to these relations of cause and effect unless we can establish our chronological sequences with some security, and in the realm of popular thought and feeling it is difficult to date most of the phenomena. It is difficult even when a country has an abundant literature, and certainly the United States of 1783 was far from literary. In the main its population was inarticulate, and the few who wrote were as likely to be expressing thoughts which they had found in European books as thoughts which originated or were current among American minds.

Again, many movements which we may trace in American thought and feeling, and which we may ascribe to the influence of the American Revolution on the principle of *post hoc, propter hoc*, may have been due to causes of worldwide range, operative in Europe quite as much as in America, with effects perceptible in countries that had had nothing to do with the American Revolution. Of the waves of thought and feeling that in past times have disturbed Europe, the most important have not failed to cross the Atlantic, though often they have arrived on these shores so transformed as not to be at once recognized. If, for instance, we compare the European revolutionary movements of 1830 and those of 1848, we perceive that they were strikingly different in character. The animating cause of the revolutions of 1830 was social discontent, that of the revolutions of 1848 was the sentiment of nationalism. Now what do we see on this side of the water? No revolutions, in either year. But in the early 'thirties we see abundant evidences of social ferment—transcendentalism and socialism, antislavery agitation and Mormonism, passionate advocacy of Graham bread and this or that medical panacea, wild financial as well as philosophical speculation, workingmen's parties, free love, and a tendency toward riots. Plainly all this constituted the American phase of the revolutionary ferment of 1830.

In 1848, on the other hand, we see in the United States no revolutions indeed, but all the symptoms of heightened nationalism—the war with Mexico, the threat of war with Great Britain, the fervor of annexationism, the proclaiming of "Manifest Destiny," the height of spread-eagle oratory—all those phenomena, in short, which led the late Professor Dunning to give to his chapter on this period the expressive title of "The Roaring Forties."

Going further back, I do not think it fantastic to discover an American phase of that modulation of key in the intellectual life of Europe, at the end of the eighteenth century and the beginning of the nineteenth, which we call the Romantic Movement. We should hardly look for many literary manifestations of it, in a land so little literary, but we may rightly see its out-croppings in the religious movements typified in the emotional revivals which in just those years stirred so deeply the forest communities of the West.

We shall, then, in any consideration of the American Revolution as a source of change in American thought and feeling, make large allowance for the working of causes that were nowise confined to the United States, for influences that, in all countries, were in the air during the years in question. Thus, it would be pleasant to think that humane influences playing about the Revolution were the cause of the movement toward prison reform of which the serious beginning may be found in the formation in 1787 of the "Philadelphia Society for Alleviating the Miseries of Public Prisons." It is true that the Americans were, as I think they still are, some-what more humane than most other peoples, and an English historian justly commends in particular the humanity with which they conducted the Revolutionary War. Their criminal code was far less savage than that of England, where when our Revolution opened two hundred offenses were punishable with death; in none of the American colonies did the number exceed twenty, and two states, Virginia and Pennsylvania, considerably softened their penal codes within our period. Four of the states ameliorated their laws respecting the imprison-ment of poor debtors, under which half the population of a prison sometimes consisted of that class and a case is recorded where seven of them were kept in prison for debts aggregating less than seven pounds.

The Revolution may have had something to do with such legislation, for the changes of fortune incident to a wildly fluctuating currency and a period of exceptional speculation probably brought into the debtors' prisons a new class of unfortunates, embracing many persons of whom legislators had personal knowledge, bringing personal compassion. Also, the frequent passage of stay-laws during the war and in the years immediately following it may have caused a more lenient feeling toward debtors to prevail. When, however, we consider how slowly the amelioration of prisons and of the penal code and of the condition of debtors proceeded, and in how few states before the end of the century, it is more reasonable to attribute what progress was made, here as in Europe, rather to the writings of Beccaria and the labors of John Howard, or in general terms to the *Zeitgeist*, than to any supposed influence of our Revolution.

On the other hand, many immediate influences from the Revolution can be securely traced. In the first place, the mere fact of independence caused the American to think and feel differently about America. Joel Barlow's *Vision of Columbus*, or President Stiles's celebrated election sermon on *The United States elevated to Glory and Honor*, could not possibly have been written twenty years earlier. Rather oddly to modern apprehension, but naturally enough when the political circumstances of the time are considered, in many cases it is the elevation of his colony to the position of an independent or sovereign state that seems to affect the citizen's mind with pride, rather than any larger aspect of independence. An evidence of this heightening of state pride may be seen in the fact that—Virginia, Massachusetts, Jamaica, New York, and New Jersey having, to be sure, already provided themselves with good colonial histories—writers in the younger and smaller states proceeded in just these years after the Revolution to prepare excellent histories of their respective states: Belknap's *New Hampshire*, Ramsay's *South Carolina*, Williamson's *North Carolina*, Proud's *Pennsylvania*, Trumbull's *Connecticut*, and the unfinished and unpublished histories of Rhode Island and of Georgia by Theodore Foster and Edward Langworthy.

Our own generation is abundantly familiar with the legacy which war leaves behind it in the form of what is called post-war psychology. The types of its manifestation are recurrent. The profiteer, the *nouveau riche*, the *Incroyable*, the flapper, are found, under varying designations, alike in 1784 or in 1796 or in 1816 or in 1866 or in 1919. Sober Americans of 1784 lamented the spirit of speculation which war and its attendant disturbances had generated, the restlessness of the young, their disrespect for tradition and authority, the increase of crime, the frivolity and extravagance of society.

There were more specific sequelae of warfare. There was the duel, for instance. Before the French and Indian War there had been few instances of it in America. Contact with British officers in that war had shown young American officers that the duel was the hallmark of military sophistication. Contact with French officers during the Revolutionary War fastened in the minds of young American officers, from whom it spread to many others, the belief that, if greatly displeased with the conduct of a fellow-citizen toward you, your proper course was to offer him an opportunity to kill you. This fantastic but not ignoble superstition persisted in many parts of America almost till the Civil War, and its upholders were as certain as Moltke was concerning warfare, that its abandonment would entail the decay of manliness.

A still larger mental effect of the Revolutionary War was the high place of political and social influence accorded, for many years after its successful conclusion, to military men who had taken part in it. Throughout history, this has been one of the stock results of warfare. All will remember our twelve soldier-presidents, and the older among us will remember how, for thirty years after the Civil War, there was no qualification for civil office, or at any rate, no qualification for candidacy, more valuable than a military title derived from that conflict. So it was with the Revolutionary War, and even more so, for, it should be remembered, to the minds of that time our national history began with the Revolution. When one went back beyond the year 1775, he lost himself in the confusion of thirteen separate streams. Therefore the men who had made the Revolutionary War successful were like the eponymous heroes who had founded Grecian cities. They had begun the history of a nation, and were entitled to an exceptional share of military glory.

The circumstances of warfare in those days, it should also be remembered, were such as lent themselves readily to the acquirement of military glory. The weapons were of short range. Battles were fought by daylight. The numbers engaged were so moderate, the field of each battle was so little extended, that the display of individual valor could be frequent and conspicuous. In such respects, the character of military struggles changed little from the time of Hector and Agamemnon till the latter years of the nineteenth century. When Horatius smote down Astur, when Ney led in person the last charge of the Guards at Waterloo, or when Armistead and Garnett at Gettysburg fell at the head of their brigades, whole armies saw and remembered. Throughout all these years military glory was within the grasp of every officer. Now, when armies in trenches and dugouts, or in the darkness of midnight, contend against invisible enemies miles away in front, and the proper post of a general officer is at the telephone instrument, miles in the rear, the opportunity to acquire personal fame in warfare has almost disappeared. The officer who passionately desires the limelight cannot obtain it by visible exploits against the enemy in the open field, but only by attacking his superiors in the front pages of the newspapers.

It would seem too large a digression if one were to discuss at length the effects of this disappearance or almost entire reduction of the soldier's opportunity for individual fame, but in passing one may draw attention to the powerful aid it brings to the cause of the world's peace. No one can review in his mind the warlike literature of previous ages, the rhetoric of military proclamations, the animating spirit of war songs and war poems, without perceiving how strong an incitement to warfare has come from the desire and hope of military glory. Under present conditions, that whole motive has practically disappeared from the world, to the world's great benefit. Of the many noble youths who eight years ago went over to the fields of France, hardly any, I think we should all agree, were influenced by that traditional motive. Did anyone ever hear any of them use the words "glory" or "laurels" or "renown"? They went to war as to an imperative but regrettable duty that must be conscientiously performed, and the scene they saw before them was not a brilliant garden of laurels but an unattractive and prosaic sea of mud.

A hundred and fifty years ago, however, military distinction was an attractive and potent reality. Those who had attained it in the Revolutionary War received from their fellow-citizens honors and offices and influence that often were well deserved and well exercised, but in not a few cases extended much beyond the qualifications for high position or beyond the time when it could suitably be retained.

Other influences from the war sprang from the fact that it was waged with the aid of French allies. Gratitude for French aid made beloved friends of those who fifteen years before had been the enemies of all English America. French officers, usually pleased with America, charmed both American men and American women. French fashions became the vogue, and French manners had their influence. French books, especially those of Voltaire and Raynal, were sold in all the bookshops. French newspapers began a precarious existence. French army surgeons taught the medical fraternity in America much that was useful. The American Philosophical Society admitted many Frenchmen as members, and the American Academy of Arts and Sciences was founded at Boston on the model of institutions of similar purpose in France. The need of learning the French language was widely felt. Twenty-six teachers of French in the United States in 1785 are known. The College of William and Mary established a chair of that language, the first in the United States, in 1779. Harvard College the next year gave it the status of a regular though elective subject of instruction, and in 1782 arranged that freshmen and sophomores might take it instead of Hebrew.

What influence upon education in general the Revolution exercised it would be difficult to say, so various were the conditions, so little systematic the organization. The Duke of La Rochefoucauld notes already in 1794 the habit of speaking of the United States as "the most enlightened nation of the world," and he notes it with tolerance, admitting a large degree of popular intelligence. Whatever foundation the boast may have had was probably due more largely to the rapid increase of newspapers and other printing which was mentioned in the last lecture, conjoined with the quickness of mind naturally produced by pioneer life and race-mixture, than to any improvements which the period of warfare can have brought to the colonial systems of elementary or secondary education. Inevitably many schools and academies must have been broken up, and though we see evidences of much desire for educational progress, it would need much time for fruition.

In respect to college education, we can see our way somewhat more clearly. When the war opened there were in the colonies nine colleges—Harvard, the College of William and Mary, Yale, the College of New Jersey (Princeton), King's College (Columbia), the College of Philadelphia (now the University of Pennsylvania), Rhode Island College (now Brown University), Dartmouth and Queen's College (Rutgers). During the war there was no addition to this list, and indeed some of these suspended operations. But within eight years from the fall of Yorktown, the number of colleges in the country was nearly doubled, by the addition of eight new ones, chiefly founded by those religious denominations which had been actively engaged in the work of perfecting their internal organization. Of the eight, one was planted in Pennsylvania, Dickinson College, then Presbyterian; four in Maryland, Washington College at Chestertown, St. John's College at Annapolis, the Catholic college at Georgetown, and a Methodist college at Abington, burned down a few years later and never rebuilt; two in Virginia, Washington and Hampden-Sidney; and one at Charleston, South Carolina. In the next decade half-a-dozen more were founded, and, as the century turned, the ambitious American mind, full of pride and hope, began to label its infant institutions with the name of universities.

Before discussing the effects of the American Revolution upon religion, it will be useful to glance for a moment at the state and relations of the various religious bodies in the colonies at the time when the war broke out. Unamerican as the idea of religious establishment seems in our day, in nine of the colonies there was in 1770 an established church. But this meant different things in different colonies. In New Hampshire, Massachusetts and Connecticut it was the Congregational Church that was established by law and supported by general taxation, and the majority of the people belonged to it, though there were considerable numbers of Baptists, and many Episcopalians in Connecticut, Boston, and Portsmouth. Of the six colonies in which the English Church was established, there was none in which its adherents constituted a majority of the people. In Virginia it included perhaps half, the Presbyterians, Baptists, Methodists, and Moravians another half. In Maryland the dissenters were more numerous than the churchmen; in New York, New Jersey, the Carolinas, and Georgia much more numerous. In New York the English Church was established in only a few localities outside of the city, and in New Jersey it cannot properly be said to have been established at all. In all the southern colonies the whole body of the people were called upon to pay taxes for the support of the ministers of the established church, though it was the church of a minority. This was a great grievance, and was bitterly resented.

It is quite true that in the colonies south of Virginia the laws regarding tithes were not strictly regarded, and that in all colonies a practical toleration had been secured, after a long struggle. Yet much remained to make the situation of a dissenter highly uncomfortable. Take North Carolina for example. The witty Colonel Byrd said that it had "a climate where no clergyman can breathe, any more than spiders in Ireland." At the end of the colonial period, there were but six Episcopal clergymen in the province. The Presbyterians and the Moravians each were as numerous as the Anglicans, and the Quakers more so. Yet all were by law obliged to contribute to the support of the English clergymen. Governor Tryon had surely no intention of being humorous when he said to the assembly, "I profess myself a warm advocate for toleration, but I never heard of toleration in any country made use of as an argument to exempt Dissenters from bearing their share of the support of the established religion." Until 1766 it is actually true that no marriages were legal that were not solemnized by the Episcopal clergymen, and even then the privilege was extended only to the Presbyterians, and on condition that the fees went to the Anglicans. Another law forbade any man to teach school unless he were an Episcopalian, though the province was in the most abject need of education.

In Pennsylvania and in Rhode Island entire religious freedom prevailed. In the former, Quakers, Lutherans, Presbyterians, Episcopalians, Baptists, Moravians, Dunkards, Mennonites, and Catholics lived side by side without difficulty. In Rhode Island the Baptists were the leading denomination, but Quakers, Episcopalians, and Congregationalists flourished undisturbed. Taking the thirteen colonies together, the most careful enumeration (the results of which have not yet been published) gives a total of 3105 religious organizations, about a thousand each in New England, the Middle Colonies, and the South. Of these, 658 congregations were of the Congregationalist order, nearly all in New England, 543 were Presbyterian, 498 Baptist, 480 Anglican, 295 of the Society of Friends, 261 German and Dutch Reformed, 151 Lutheran, and 50 Catholic.

With all this varied mixture of religions, the shock of revolution would necessarily loosen the bonds which bound unwilling multitudes to any church establishment with which they had no sympathy. In New England the established church was not immediately threatened, for it was the church of the majority, and most of its clergy and adherents were on the American side, while its opponents were also the opponents of the Revolution. Accordingly in New Hampshire the Congregational Church continued to be established until 1817, in Connecticut till 1818, in Massachusetts even down to 1833. In the colonies where the church established by law was the Episcopal Church, disestablishment was effected with comparative ease, except in Virginia. Here the established church had perhaps as many communicants as dissenters, and it had the warm support of many influential men, some of whom doubtless felt, as did one whose opinion has been quoted and thus preserved to us: "Sure I am, that no *gentleman* will choose to go to Heaven otherwise than by the way of the established church."

Disestablishment in Virginia was a natural consequence of the doctrine laid down in the Virginia Declaration of Rights of 1776, but some difficulty was to be expected in immediately carrying out that doctrine. George Mason's original draft of that Declaration had pronounced for a complete toleration. A very young member named James Madison, who had been much impressed by the wrongs of the dissenters in concrete cases which he had known, urged something more than mere toleration, and the Declaration as finally passed read as follows. "16. That religion, or the duty which we owe to our Creator, and the manner of discharging it, can be directed only by reason and conviction, not by force or violence, and therefore all men are equally entitled to the free exercise of religion, according to the dictates of conscience, and that it is the mutual duty of all to practise Christian forbearance, love and charity towards each other."

It was asked in convention whether this was meant as a prelude to an attack on the established church, and Patrick Henry declared that it was not. Nevertheless such principles led inevitably to the equality of all religious bodies before the law, and the peculiar privileges of the established church were sure to be soon assailed. This was the more likely to happen because so many of the Episcopal clergy were Tories. Moreover, their own character was in many cases to blame for the feeling against them. Very likely the stories regarding the roystering and fox-hunting Virginia parsons of the eighteenth century are exaggerated. Probably we must not regard as typical the one who, after dinner every Sunday with the chief planter of his neighborhood, was tied in his chaise and sent home with a servant, nor that other and most humorous man of God who, after thrashing his vestry soundly, added insult to injury by preaching to them next day from the text, "And I contended with them, and cursed them, and smote certain of them, and plucked off their hair." But there is enough evidence to show that there was much looseness among the Virginian clergy, and, if not much evil living, at any rate much want of zeal. Otherwise it would be impossible to explain the rapid progress of dissent. At the beginning of the century dissenters had had no places of worship in the colony except three or four Presbyterian meeting-houses and one of the Quakers, and now half the population were dissenters. The Presbyterians were the first to become numerous and active, especially as the upland portions of the country became filled with a population of Irish or Scotch-Irish immigrants. Soon the Moravians, Baptists, and New Lights began to multiply, and Germans, Lutheran or Reformed, from Pennsylvania. The vitality of these sects was greater than that of the established church, and they rapidly gathered strength for the coming conflict, in which, too, they were sure to be aided by many Episcopal laymen whose political principles of hostility to all privileges influenced them more strongly than regard for the special interests of their church.

In the conflict that now arose, feelings of the most extreme warmth were engaged. The dissenters had received hard measure at the hands of governors and legislatures which for a long time had been almost without exception composed of Episcopalians. Actual persecutions even had been visited upon them, such as one may see recorded in the quaint and engaging narrative of Robert Semple. Marriages by their clergy were invalid. They were taxed for the support of a church concerning which it was but natural for them to feel that its services to the cause of Christianity were much less considerable than their own more enthusiastic labors. Accordingly they were eager to pull down the establishment altogether: "There had been a time," says Semple, "when they would have been satisfied, to have paid their tithes, if they could have had liberty of conscience; but now, the crisis was such, that nothing less than a total overthrow of all ecclesiastical distinctions, would satisfy their sanguine hopes. Having started the decaying edifice, every dissenter put to his shoulder, to push it into irretrievable ruin." They were sure of the most ardent support of Jefferson and of Madison.

Scarcely had the first legislature under independence begun its sessions, when petitions for religious freedom began to pour in upon it. Among them is one petition which was said to be signed by ten thousand freemen. Several thousand names still remain attached to it, and the signatures, examined with care, or indeed the very number of such signatures to this and other similar petitions, show that the dissenters were by no means an illiterate portion of the population. On the other hand there is a petition to the contrary from a considerable number of the clergy of the established church, and a Methodist petition upon the same side, signed by one of their ministers in behalf of nearly three thousand Methodists. The clergymen represent that the public faith had been virtually pledged to them for the receiving of due recompense for their services as long as they lived, that they had entered into holy orders upon that understanding and were now practically incapacitated for any other calling, and argue strongly in favor of an establishment upon grounds of public utility.

Upon the other side the ablest memorial presented was that of the chief organization of the Virginian Presbyterians, the celebrated Hanover Presbytery. Baptists and Quakers and Mennonites joined with them. The struggle which followed was afterward characterized by Jefferson, who had surely seen many political struggles, as the severest he had ever witnessed. The issue of it was the passage of an act by which dissenters were exempted from taxes for the support of the established church. It was made lawful for ministers of other churches to celebrate the rite of marriage. All acts for providing the salaries of the clergy were suspended. It was thought that, as a possible solution of the matter, a general tax might be levied for the support of religion, but each taxpayer be left free to declare to which religious body his taxes should be turned over. Patrick Henry favored this, and so, I believe, did General Washington. But the plan was postponed till after the Revolution, and then failed. Instead, Mr. Jefferson succeeded in securing the passage of his act for establishing religious freedom, of which he was so proud that he ordered the inscription on his grave-stone to read: "Thomas Jefferson, Author of the Declaration of American Independence, of the Statute of Virginia for Religious Freedom, and Father of the University of Virginia." This statute, after a highly rhetorical preamble, characteristic of Mr. Jefferson, provides that "no man shall be compelled to frequent or support any religious worship, place, or ministry whatsoever; nor shall be enforced, restrained, molested, or burdened in his body or goods, nor shall otherwise suffer on account of his religious opinions or belief; but that all men shall be free to profess, and by argument to maintain, their opinions in matters of religion."

In Maryland, in New York, and in the southernmost colonies the Anglican Church was disestablished early in the Revolutionary contest, and with comparatively little difficulty. Everywhere it involved a large measure of hardship to certain individuals, but surely no one can be sorry that the system of voluntary support took the place of legal compulsion, especially of legal compulsion to support an unacceptable church. If religious freedom and equality is America's chief contribution to the world's civilization, as has been conspicuously declared—and surely much could be said for this view—great honor belongs to the men of the Revolutionary period, for then it was, more than at any other time, that this principle, so distinctive of America and so invaluable to her prosperity and development, was put into actual practice.

It would be absurd to affirm, however, that religious freedom and equality had yet reached their full development in America. In three of the four New England states, the Congregational churches continued to be established. In Massachusetts and Maryland no man could take any office without subscribing a declaration that he believed in the Christian religion. In Pennsylvania he must also declare (and this applied to all members of the legislature also) that he believed the Scriptures to be given by divine inspiration. Delaware

required a Trinitarian test for both officers and legislators. In New Jersey, North Carolina, and South Carolina, they must be Protestants. "No person," says the
constitution of North Carolina, "who shall deny the
being of God, or the truth of the Protestant religion, or
the divine authority either of the Old or New Testa-
ments, or who shall hold religious principles incom-
patible with the freedom or safety of the State, shall be
capable of holding any office or place of trust or profit
in the civil department within this State." Yet in most
cases these restrictions disappeared before many years,
and substantially the battle of religious liberty was won.

So far we have been speaking of positive gains which
came to American religion by means of the Revolution.
It is not to be supposed that there were not also losses.
Many writers agree in declaring that service in the
patriotic army was naturally demoralizing. Outside the
army, too, attention was turned away from religious
things. Congregations were broken up. In many cases
their ministers went to the war as chaplains, or fled to
the enemy as Tories. Sometimes they entered on more
belligerent service. Two of the Episcopal clergymen of
Virginia became colonels in the Revolutionary army,
and one of them became a brigadier-general.

Many churches were destroyed, injured, or desecrated
during the war. The Old South Church in Boston was
used as a riding-school by the British cavalry. So was
one of the Dutch Reformed churches in New York City,
while another was used as a hospital. Presbyterian
churches suffered especially, for the Presbyterians were
almost all Whigs. Indeed, it is said that if the British
soldiers discovered a large Bible and a metrical version
of the psalms of David in any house, they took it as

prima facie evidence that it was the home of a rebel. The Presbyterian church at Newtown, Long Island, had its steeple sawed off, and was used as a prison and guardhouse till it was torn down and its boards used for the construction of soldiers' huts. That at Crumpond was burned to save it from being occupied by the enemy. That of Mount Holly was burned. That of Princeton was seized by the Hessians, and stripped of its pews and gallery for fuel. A fireplace was built in it, and a chimney carried up through the roof. Washington, supposing that it would be defended against him, planted his cannon near it and began firing into it. The church at Babylon, Long Island, was torn down by the enemy for military purposes. That of Elizabeth was burned. The Presbyterian churches in New York City were made into prisons, or used by the British officers for stabling their horses. More than fifty places of worship in various parts of the country were entirely destroyed by the enemy during the course of the war. Even where the church-edifice was unharmed, the congregation was often scattered. Thus, at Albany, which suffered little from the war, Presbyterian services almost altogether ceased, and with the return of peace the church had to be organized anew. On the other hand Episcopal churches were likely to suffer because of the Toryism of their pastors or people.

Even if no harm were intentionally done, it was likely that, in a country having but few large public buildings of any other kind, churches would be pressed into service as hospitals, barracks, and storehouses, and thus exposed to destruction in greater measure than usual. Our heroic ancestors, it will be remembered, scorned the effeminacy of warming their churches, so that the chance of their burning down was not great. Military uses increased this chance immediately.

In Maryland and Virginia war and disestablishment operated together to disorganize the Anglican Church. When the Revolution broke out, there were in Maryland forty-four parishes and forty-four incumbents. When it closed, but eighteen or twenty rectors remained. In Virginia there had been ninety-five parishes, one hundred and four churches and chapels, and ninety-one clergymen of the established church. When the contest was over, a large number of the churches were found to be destroyed or injured beyond repairing. The reader of good Bishop Meade's interesting old book on the old churches, ministers, and families of Virginia will remember how often he laments the continued disuse and disrepair of churches which fell into dilapidation at the time of the Revolution. Of the ninety-five parishes, twenty-three were extinct or forsaken when the war ended, and thirty-four more were without ministerial services. Of the ninety-one clergymen only twenty-eight remained who had weathered the storm, and of these, only fifteen continued in the same churches which they had occupied before the Revolution. Thirteen had been driven by violence or want from their old parishes but had found a refuge in some other parish which happened to be vacant and was perhaps less reduced by the war. For many years after the war, the church was at a low ebb in Virginia. Bishop Meade tells us that when he was ordained at Williamsburg, one Sunday in winter, as the Bishop and he were making their way to the old church, they met a number of the students of William and Mary College with guns on their shoulders and dogs at their sides going out hunting, while at the same time one of the citizens was filling his ice-house. The windows of the church were broken, and the congregation consisted of two ladies and about fifteen gentlemen. In Richmond, for several years after the war, the church was seldom used, and the only religious services held, in a population amounting to three or four thousand, were Episcopal and Presbyterian services held on alternate Sundays in a room in the state capitol.

Nor was this deadness confined to the Episcopal Church, in which case it might possibly be attributed to the losses which that church had suffered through disestablishment. Travellers as various as the royalist French Duke of La Rochefoucauld, the republican Brissot de Warville, the English manufacturer Henry Wansey all unite in testifying to it as common among the Congregationalists and Presbyterians as well, in Boston, in New York, and in Philadelphia. The old historian of the Virginia Baptists tells us, in quaint phrases, that "the war, though very propitious to the liberty of the Baptists, had an opposite effect upon the life of religion among them. From whatever cause," he says, "certain it is, that they suffered a very wintry season. With some few exceptions, the declension was general throughout the state. The love of many waxed cold. Some of the watchmen fell, others stumbled, and many slumbered at their posts. Iniquity greatly abounded." There is much to support what the famous Marquis of Pescara said to the papal legate, "It is impossible for men to serve Mars and Christ at the same time." It is possible for individuals, but it is difficult for a whole generation.

However great the apathy which had fallen upon the spirit of American religion, it would surely recover, as the nation itself gradually recovered from the ravages and injuries of war. A nation inspired by the sense of a career of future greatness can seldom fail to develop active religious life in some form, and it was certain that America would sometime become religious, even if it were not so in the years immediately after the Revolution. Meanwhile it was possible for it to be developing its ecclesiastical systems, and indeed natural for it to do so. The whole period from the close of the war to the year 1789 was, it is familiar, a period of constitution-making in the United States. It is perhaps less familiar that this period of activity in the making of constitutions for civil government was also marked by great activity in the framing of constitutions for ecclesiastical government. The complete separation of church and state in America, and our division into numerous denominations, should not blind us to the fact that there is after all a certain unity in American church history, as well as a frequent connection between it and the civil history of the nation. Whether this can be made out at other times or not, it certainly can be seen at the particular period we are considering. The great fact of national independence forced several churches to recast their forms of government, and the occupation of men's minds with problems of national organization could not fail to stir them up to improvements in their religious organization, in a country where, as in America, the clergy were far from being a class apart, uninfluenced by what was going on around them and totally separate from the laity.

Let us begin with the Episcopal Church. If it had really needed a bishop before the war—and about this there had been an agitation that alarmed many members of other churches—how much more now! It was not possible that the independent United States of America should continue to be a part of the diocese of the bishop of London. It was not possible that the ministers of that church should go on reading the prayers for King George and the other parts of the service which assumed a monarchical government. So began the movement for an American episcopate. That political grounds had had the chief part in the previous opposition to this movement, is shown by the fact that there was no opposition now. But how to secure the ordination of bishops was a question of much difficulty. Indeed it now seemed impossible to obtain from England the ordination of priests even. Dr. Franklin, with his curious inability to perceive religious distinctions, made an amusing attempt, through the papal nuncio in Paris, to see if a young correspondent of his could not be ordained in the Catholic Church without becoming a member of its communion. Adams made a more promising attempt to obtain for such young men an ordination through the Danish bishops. The King of Denmark was found willing. But meantime the movement for an American episcopate came rapidly forward. Bishop Seabury was consecrated by the non-juring Scottish bishops. A meeting of the clergy at New York in 1784 began the framing of a constitution for the Protestant Episcopal Church in America. Just as in the case of the Constitution of the United States, inter-state jealousies hindered union. But, by a somewhat similar process, conventions held at Philadelphia in 1785, 1786, and 1789 adjusted all differences, and united in a federal union the various dioceses, as the various states were being united in the more famous federal union of the United States. In the maintenance of the state system, in the relations of the two houses in the General Convention, and in many minor details, the constitution adopted for the church showed the influence of the Constitution just adopted for the civil government of the country.

Another church which was obliged to place itself upon a new basis was the Catholic Church. Hitherto the Catholic clergy in America had been under the control of the vicar apostolic of London. But when Great Britain had acknowledged the independence of the United States, the new vicar apostolic of London disclaimed all jurisdiction over them, and candidates for orders found themselves in the same predicament as the young Episcopalians. The Catholic clergy met in Maryland in 1783 and discussed plans of organization. In France there was some talk of their being annexed to a French vicariate apostolic. But more judicious counsels prevailed at Rome, and in 1784 the Catholic Church in the United States was by decree of the Congregation of the Propaganda erected into a distinct body, with Father John Carroll, cousin of Charles Carroll of Carrollton, as prefect apostolic. Later, in 1790, he was made bishop of Baltimore, and the new organization of the Catholic Church in America was complete.

So entirely had the Methodist body in America been under the control of John Wesley that, among them also, the fact of American independence made necessary a radical change of organization. In 1773, when the first American Methodist conference was held, the society had ten circuits and sixteen hundred members. In 1783, in spite of the prevailing apathy in other religious bodies, they were five times as numerous, and it became difficult to keep them to certain of Wesley's rules. Wesley always wished his followers to remain in the Church of England, but the American Methodists often found it impossible to receive the communion or to obtain the baptism of their children if they must depend on the Episcopal clergymen. Wesley, therefore, after much hesitation, consecrated Thomas Coke as superintendent of the American Methodists, with powers of ordination, and assigned the same position to Francis Asbury. At the famous Christmas Conference held at Baltimore in 1784 Asbury was ordained, and an independent organization set in operation for the Methodist Church in the United States. Presently the title of "bishop" superseded that of "superintendent." The society dropped from its minutes that curious clause, which paints to the life the spirit of the earliest Methodism: "During the life of the Rev. Mr. Wesley, we acknowledge ourselves his sons in the gospel, ready, in matters belonging to church government, to obey his commands." The general conferences gradually gave more and more settled shape to the internal regulations of the society, till finally it had perfected its organization as an independent American church.

Other religious bodies felt less pressure than these from the mere fact of independence to give themselves new form. But the constitution-making spirit was in the air, and hardly any escaped it. One denomination after another took on a more comprehensive or more highly developed organization. The main body of the Presbyterians in 1788 provided for this completer development, and in 1789 the first General Assembly of the Presbyterian Church in the United States convened at Philadelphia. The Dutch Reformed Church, which had obtained its independence of Europe before the Revolution began, held its first General Synod in 1792. Even the seceding Presbyterians of the strict Covenanting school attempted in 1782 to unite, though, unhappily yet characteristically, the attempt only resulted in the production of three bodies in the place of two. The Freewill Baptists set up a yearly meeting in 1792. The Universalists held their first general convention in 1786. The United Brethren in Christ held their first formal conference at Baltimore in 1789. Even the Baptists, whose plan of independent congregations lent itself ill to superior organization, instituted in Virginia, in 1784, a General Committee to act for the whole in certain matters. In short, there was no important religious body, except the Congregationalists, which did not, in just these years, go through something of this process. Evidently there was no escaping the general impulse which in those years was leading the Americans, in all possible ways, to draw together in better forms of organization.

In the election sermon already alluded to, preached by President Stiles before the General Assembly of Connecticut in 1783, the preacher makes plain his expectation that the future of religion in the United States will belong, not far from equally, to the three denominations of the Congregationalists, the Presbyterians, and the Episcopalians. Great would be his astonishment could he see the numerical proportions in our day, the first, second, and third places occupied by the Catholics, Methodists, and Baptists, of whom he made little account, the denominations which ranked foremost in his prophecy now standing eighth, fourth, and seventh. He could not foresee the workings of democracy and immigration, and failed to imagine that the future in such a country would fall, not to denominations whose traditions required an educated and therefore expensive ministry, but to those whose system could be flexibly adapted to the conditions of frontier settlement.

It is not intended in these lectures, nor is the lecturer competent, to discuss at length the influence of the Revolution upon theological thought in the United States. But I will, in mere passing mention, call attention to the fact that, of the religious bodies which in this period were growing in numbers and zeal, four (that is to say, all but one) were anti-Calvinistic—namely, the Methodists, the Universalists, the Unitarians, and the Freewill Baptists. This is not without significance. In a period when the special privileges of individuals were being called in question or destroyed, there would naturally be less favor for that form of theology which was dominated by the doctrine of the especial election of a part of mankind, a growing favor for those forms which seemed more distinctly to be based upon the idea of the natural equality of all men. But I dwell upon the thought no farther than to bring it forward as one more illustration of that general thesis which in fact underlies this whole series of lectures—the thesis that all the varied activities of men in the same country and period have intimate relations with each other, and that one cannot obtain a satisfactory view of any one of them by considering it apart from the others.

INDEX

Adams, John, 14, 66, 96
Agriculture: in colonies, 28–29, 50; experimentation in, 49–52; societies for promotion of, 51–52
Alfred, King, 48
American Academy of Arts and Sciences, 81
American Association, 69
American Philosophical Society, 81
American Revolution: centennial observances of, 3; changing view of, 4–7; aims of, 8; compared with French Revolution, 8–9, 15; trade restrictions as cause of, 13; supporters of, analyzed, 13–18; age of leaders in, 15; size of colonial army in, 48
— effects of: social, 18–19, 26; on slavery, 21–26; economic, 32–46; on land ownership, 32–33; on land laws, 36–38; on industry, 52–59; on commerce, 62–63, 69–71, 72–73; on humanitarianism, 76–77; on dueling, 78; on military prestige, 79; on education, 82–83; on religion, 83–100; on theological thought, 100
Ames, Fisher, 61
Annapolis Convention (1786), 72
Anti-slavery societies, 23–24
Asbury, Francis, 98

Bank of New York, 64
Bank of North America, 63–64
Baptists: in trans-Allegheny West, 44; in colonies, 83, 85, 87; opposed to establishment, 89; postwar decline in church attendance, 94; organizational changes by, 99
Barlow, Joel, 77
Beccaria, Cesare Bonesana, 77
Belknap, Jeremy, 19
Benezet, Anthony, 22
Brandywine Creek, 60
Brandywine, battle of, 57
Brissot de Warville, Jacques Pierre, 68, 94
Buffon, Comte de, 51
Burke, Edmund, 8–9
Byrd, Colonel, 84

Carroll, Charles, of Carrollton, 18, 97
Carroll, Rev. John, 97
Catholics: in colonies, 85; organizational changes by, 97; numerical proportions of, 98
China trade, 68–69
Christmas Conference (Baltimore, 1784), 98
Churches: damaged in war, 91–93; changes in constitutions and organization of, 95–99
Civil War: shift in power during, 11; percentage of population involved in, 47–48; economic benefits from, 72–73

Coke, Thomas, 98
Collot-d'Herbois, Jean Marie, 15
Colonization, 29, 32
Commerce: effects of Revolution on, 62–63, 69–71, 72–73; maritime, 64–67; hampered by weak government, 71–72; regulation of, 72
Committees of Safety, 56
Congregationalists: in colonies, 83, 85; postwar decline in church attendance, 94; numerical proportions of, 99
Connecticut: slavery in, 22, 24, 25; boundary dispute of, 43; agricultural society formed, 51; and Congregational Church, 83, 85
Constitution, U.S., 36, 72
Continental Congress, 7; and slave trade, 24; and manufacturing, 55; and munitions, 56–57; and postwar inflation, 62; and regulation of commerce, 69
Cooper, Dr. Thomas, 52, 60
Couthon, Georges, 15
Coxe, Tench, 69
Cromwell, Oliver, 12

Danton, Georges Jacques, 15
Daughters of the American Revolution, 3
Debtors laws, 76–77
Declaration of Independence, 69
DeLancey, James, 35
Delaware: and slavery, 24–25; religious test for office in, 91
Democracy: economic, 27–28; political, 27, 39, 46; social, 39, 46
Desmoulins, Camille, 15
DeWitt, General Simeon, 42
Disestablishment, 85–86, 90, 93
Dudley, Lord, 61
Dueling, 78
Dunkards, 57, 85

Dutch Reformed Church: in trans-Allegheny West, 44; in colonies, 85; first General Synod of, 98–99
Dutch West India Company, 30

Election laws, 40–41
Eliot, Rev. Jared, 50
Entails: purpose of, 36–37; abolition of, 37–39
Episcopalians: as Tories, 13–14; in colonies, 83, 84, 85; decline in postwar attendance, 93–94; organizational changes by, 96–97; numerical proportions of, 99
Essex, Earl of, 12
Evans, Oliver, 56

Fairfax estate (Virginia), 31, 35
Fox's Book of Martyrs, 57
Franklin, Benjamin, 28–29, 96
Freewill Baptists, 99, 100. See also Baptists
French influence, 81
French Revolution: change in attitude toward, 7–8; compared with American Revolution, 8–9; shift in control of, 12

Galloway, Joseph, 14
Geography: of Atlantic Coast, 30–31; effect of, on settlement, 30–32
Georgia: land confiscations by, 35; land laws in, 37; religion in, 83
Granville, Lord, 31
Great Britain, 7, 9
Green, Captain John, 68

Hampden, John, 12
Hanover Presbytery, 89
Harvard College, 81
Henry, Patrick: opposed to slavery, 22–23; and religious freedom, 86, 89

INDEX

Howard, John, 77
Howe, General William, 16
Humanitarianism, 22, 76–77
Hume, David, 14

Immigrants, 14–15
Inflation, 62
Iron industry, 53

Jarratt, Rev. Devereux, 19–20
Jay, John, 24
Jefferson, Thomas, 38, 51, 88, 89–90
Johnson, Sir John, 35

Kentucky, 43–45

Lafayette, Marquis de, 55
Land: changes in distribution of, 32–33; speculation in, 41
Land laws: and royal restrictions, 32; postwar changes in, 36–38
La Rochefoucauld-Liancourt, Duke of, 41, 58, 60, 82, 94
Loyalists, 19. See also Tories
Lutherans, 87

Madison, James, 86, 88
Magazine of American History, 3
Manchester, Earl of, 12
Manufacturing: effect of Revolution on, 52–53; restrictions on, 52–54; encouraged by Continental Congress, 55; of woolen goods, 55; of textile machinery, 56; of munitions, 56; of paper, 58; of salt, 58; of ships, 59; postwar, 60; domestic, 60–61
Maryland: slavery in, 21; anti-slavery society formed in, 24; slave trade banned, 25; Tory property confiscated, 35; regulation of commerce by, 72; religion in, 83; religious test

for office in, 90; disestablishment in, 90, 93
Mason, George, 86
Massachusetts: Superior Court of, 14, 25; slavery in, 22, 25; Tory property confiscated in, 34; boundary dispute of, 42–43; agricultural society formed in, 51; domestic manufacturing in, 61; privateering in, 66; and Congregational Church, 83, 85; religious test for office in, 90
Massachusetts Bank, 64
Meade, Bishop, 93, 94
Mennonites, 85, 89
Methodists: and establishment, 89; organizational changes by, 97–98; numerical proportions of, 99; growth of, 100
Moravians, 83–87
Morris, Robert, 35, 64, 66
Munitions industry, 56–57

Navigation Acts, 64, 69
New England: Tory evacuation of, 16; economy of, 28–29; geography of, 30–31; wool industry in, 52–53. See also Connecticut; Massachusetts; New Hampshire; Vermont
New Hampshire: Tory estates confiscated by, 34; boundary dispute of, 43; Congregational Church in, 83, 85
New Jersey: slavery in, 22; anti-slavery society formed in, 24; land laws in, 37; religion in, 83, 84; religious test for office in, 91
New Lights, 87
New York: Tories in, 16; slavery in, 22; anti-slavery society formed in, 23–24; manorial grants in, 31; royalist property confiscated in, 34; land laws in, 37; election laws

changed in, 40; land speculation in, 41–42; agricultural
society formed in, 51; and
Anglican Church, 83–84; disestablishment in, 90
Newspapers, 58
North Carolina: suffrage qualifications in, 20; slavery in, 21,
25; land laws in, 37; religion
in, 84; religious test for office
in, 91
Northwest Territory, 45

Ohio Company, 45
Ohio River, 44, 45
Otis, James, 14

Paine, Thomas, 64
Paper industry, 58
Parliament, British: and compen-
sation to Loyalists, 35; and
colonial manufactures, 52–54
Parliamentary Reform Act
(1832), 11
Parsons, Ebenezer, 68–69
Patriotism, 4, 5
Payne, Thomas, 39
Pepperrell, William, 34
Penn estate, 34
Penn, Richard, Governor, 56
Pennsylvania: Tory sympathies
in, 15, 17; slavery in, 22, 25;
Tory property confiscated in,
34; boundary disputes of, 43;
agricultural society formed
in, 51; religious freedom in,
85; religious test for office in,
90
Philadelphia Convention (1787),
72
Potter, Captain Simeon, 65
Presbyterians: in trans-Allegheny
West, 44; in colonies, 83–89;
opposed to establishment, 89;
as Whigs, 91–92; church
buildings injured, 91–92; postwar decline in attendance, 94;

organizational changes by, 98,
99; numerical proportions of,
99
Primogeniture: abolition of, 20,
37; purpose of, 36–37
Prison reform, 76
Privateering, 64–67
Protestant Episcopal Church, 97.
See also Episcopalians
Pym, John, 12

Quakers: in colonies, 84, 85; and
establishment, 89
Quebec Act (1774), 32
Quincy, Josiah, 15
Quincy, Samuel, 15
Quit-rents, 33

Ramsay, Dr. David, 17
Randolph, Edmund, 15
Randolph, Sir John, 15
Redemptioners, 21
Religion: in colonies, 83–85;
effect of Revolution on, 85–
100
Religious tests for office, 90–91
Revolutions: political, 10; popu-
lar, 10–11; natural sequence
in, 10–12. See also American
Revolution; French Revolu-
tion
Rhode Island: slavery in, 22;
anti-slavery society formed in,
24; abolition movement in, 24,
25, 68; religious freedom in,
85
Ripley, Dr. Ezra, 63
Robespierre, M. de, 15
Rousseau, Jean Jacques, 22

St. Eustatius (island), 69, 70
Saint-Just, Louis de, 15
Salt industry, 58–59
Scotch-Irish, 14–15
Seabury, Samuel, Bishop, 96
Shipbuilding, 59
Skinner, William, 39

Slave trade: restrictions on, 23, 24–25, 67–68; postwar revival of, 67–68

Slavery: and revolutionary ideals, 21; societies for alleviation of, 23–24; restrictions on, 23, 24–25, 67–68; state abolition of, 24–26

Society for Promoting the Manumission of Slaves, 23–24

Society for the Promotion of Agriculture, 51

Society for the Relief of Free Negroes Unlawfully Held in Bondage, 23

Society of Friends, 23

South Carolina: Tories in, 17; slavery in, 21, 25, 67; agricultural society formed in, 51; religious test for office in, 91

Stamp Act, 14

Stiles, Ezra, 77, 99–100

Suffrage: expansion of, 18–20; as measure of democracy, 28; property qualifications for, 39

Supreme Court (U.S.), 36

Tennessee, 44

Thucydides, 17–18

Tithes, 84

Tories: analyzed by classes, 13–17; evacuation of, 16; estates of, confiscated, 34–36

Townshend Acts, 54

Tryon, William, 84

Tyler, Moses Coit, 42

Unitarians, 100

United Brethren in Christ, 99

Universalists, 99, 100

Valley Forge, 6

Van Rensselaer manor, 31

Vermont, 25

Virginia: political attitudes in, 17; slavery in, 21, 25–26; geography of, 30–31; land laws in, 37, 38; franchise in, 39; and settlement of Kentucky, 44; domestic manufacturing in, 60–61; and regulation of commerce, 72; and Anglican church, 83; disestablishment in, 85–86, 87, 93

Virginia Convention (1774), 55

Virginia Declaration of Rights (1776), 86

Virginia Statute for Religious Freedom, 89–90

Voltaire, 22

Wansey, Henry, 41–42, 94

Warfare, changes in, 47–48

Washington, George, 18, 48, 89

Wentworth, John, 34

Wesley, John, 22, 97–98

Westward expansion, 43–46

Whigs, 13–18

Whipple, Abraham, 66

Whitefield, George, 22

Whittemore, Amos, 56

Wilderness Road, 44

William and Mary College, 81, 93

Wool industry, 52–53, 55, 56

Wright, Sir James, 35